A HARLEY
OR *My Wife*

A Guide for Midlife Men
(and the women who love them)

Noel McNaughton

A Harley or My Wife

For information address Caboodle Publishing at P.O. 460303, Centennial, CO 80046-0303.

This publication is designed to provide information in regard to the subject matter covered. In so doing, neither the publisher nor the author is engaged in rendering legal, accounting or other professional services. If you require legal advice or other expert assistance, you should seek the services of a professional specializing in the particular discipline required.

While the author has made every effort to provide accurate information at the time of publication, neither the publisher nor the author assumes any responsibility for errors, or for changes that occur after publication.

Caboodle Publishing books may be purchased for educational, business or sales promotional use. For information, please write:

Special Promotions Department, Caboodle Publishing, P.O. Box 460303, Centennial, CO 80046-0303.

SECOND EDITION

Published by Caboodle Publishing, Denver, CO – www.caboodlepublishing.com

Edited by Bobbi Trammell

Cover Design by Scott Wold

ISBN 13: 978-0-9788799-7-6
ISBN 10: 0-9788799-7-X

10 9 8 7 6 5 4 3 2 1

155.66
mc

Table of Contents

Introduction

Welcome to this book. I am glad you have it in your hands, and I hope it helps you on your journey now that you are in your middle years.

I have had MANY emails from women wondering what is happening to their men. They tell me their husbands were loving and kind and happy for twenty (more or less) years and they have suddenly become sullen, uncommunicative, and angry. Many of the women who write say their husbands have left, they don't know why, and they wonder how to get them back.

The men who write me are struggling with change in their lives.

They ask questions such as:

- Why don't I care about what I used to be passionate about?
- Where is the meaning in my life?
- Why do I feel so down, when everything looks like it should be up?
- What's happening with my marriage?
- Why don't I get turned on with my wife anymore?
- Why doesn't my wife want to be with me?
- What does my wife want from me?
- Where did all my energy go?
- Why can't I concentrate any more?
- Why do I feel more emotional about everything?
- Why do I get angry so quickly these days?
- Where did this lethargy come from?

You have probably noticed some other changes too.

- You're taking longer to recover from injuries and illness.
- You've noticed you don't have as much physical stamina as you used to have.
- You've put on a few pounds, and are feeling a little overweight.
- You've had to get reading glasses to make out the small print, and you're getting so forgetful, you can't remember where you put them.
- You are feeling anxious about the future, or maybe you are just generally anxious and don't know exactly why.
- You're feeling a little depressed, or maybe you have had a bout of clinical depression.
- You can't seem to make decisions as easily as you used to, and you have lost some confidence in your abilities. Life isn't as much fun as it used to be.
- You have started to question the value of what you do for a living, and can't think of what would fire your passion.
- You are not as interested in sex as you used to be, and you have experienced some changes in your sexuality that is worrying you.
- Sex with your partner isn't as exciting as it used to be, and you find yourself daydreaming about having sex with other women, and are maybe masturbating more, and finding it more satisfying because you don't have to worry about not performing well.
- You are having some problems in your marriage, or maybe you have recently been separated or divorced.
- You feel as though you are dead inside, that the juice in your life is gone.

If any of this sounds familiar, this book will help you.

Midlife is not just a 'thing we go through'. It is a major transition into a different stage of life. Our values change, our energy changes, and we get our first glimpse of the 'end of the road.'

It can be a time of great upheaval in our lives, and if we don't approach it in the right way, we can create quite a wreck. If we do approach this transition properly, we can come out the other side with richer, more satisfying lives.

If you have been struggling with changes you don't understand, and you feel as though you are wandering in the wilderness, you are not alone. Millions of other men are struggling just like you are. The problem we men have is that we all think we are the only ones this is happening to, so we don't think to look for help or solace from our brothers who are on the same road, or who have finished the trip, and can tell us the potholes and pitfalls to watch out for.

Another problem we men have is that we don't want to appear weak, so we don't tell anyone else about the things we are struggling with. During my early-to-mid forties, I left my job, went back to university, got divorced, started a new business, and remarried. Looking back, it looked like stereotypical midlife crisis behaviour. Only none of it felt like a crisis! Every change seemed like a good change.

My early fifties were a different story. For most of a decade, I had been passionate about teaching Holistic Management™ to farm families, and I was surprised when my passion suddenly faded. At about the same time, I began to notice I had lost energy along with my sense of life mission. I also lost confidence and libido, and went into nearly five years of mild depression. I didn't know what my life was all about any more.

I decided to do a little research and it turns out that this kind of midlife transition is as old as the human race. In hunter-gatherer societies it was recognized and honoured. Unfortunately in our 'modern' society, men struggling with this very real life process are seen to be weak or imagining things.

When I was in this transition, I would meet other men my age - such as university classmates - and when they asked how I was doing, I would actually tell them about the things I was struggling with. More often then not they would say "You too? I thought I was the only one going through that!"

So again I say: You are not alone.

I hope this book helps.
Noel

SECTION ONE
HAVE YOU LOST YOUR MIND?

Tune up your Mental Attitudes

Midlife Change: It's Real

Ever wondered whether your midlife crisis is "real" or you whether are just feeling sorry for yourself? Wonder no more. A recent study says the midlife crisis is a bona-fide condition and that 40-somethings (I would add 30-somethings, 50-somethings and even 60-somethings) all over the world struggle with it.

Researchers from Dartmouth College in Hanover, New Hampshire, and the University of Warwick in Coventry, England, combed through 35 years worth of data on two million people from 80 nations, and concluded that there is a consistent, age-related pattern in depression and happiness. We are most unhappy in midlife and happiest at either end of our lives.

This pattern of midlife misery holds true regardless of gender, education, marital status, number and age of children, occupation or income.

"The good news", according to Andrew Oswald, economics professor at the University of Warwick in Britain and co-author of the study, "is it then picks up, which means that unless lots of bad things happen to you, such as severe ill health, you'll be just as happy at 70 as you were at 20 and very possibly happier".

Oswald speculates that the midlife crisis, and subsequent happier time, occurs because people begin to bump up against their limitations and unrealistic expectations in their 30s and hit a low point in their 40s. Eventually they move through their disappointments, accept their situation as it is, and go on to feel more satisfied as they age.

What Folk Tales Have to Say About Midlife

Allan B. Chinen, who is a Jungian psychologist, wrote the book, *Once Upon A Midlife* back in the early 1990s. It is an excellent book that uses folk tales to point out ageless themes in the midlife passage. Chinen came at this in an interesting way. Here is an excerpt from an interview in M.E.N. Magazine, January, 1994:

> Chinen: It started over ten years ago, when I would be jogging, or meditating, or walking on a beach, or hiking. I got vivid images, which I realized were the endings of stories. It seemed like I needed to write the stories, rather than interpret the images. So I sat down and wrote out these stories, about how the people in the images ended up in that situation. They turned out to be fairy tales. But all the protagonists turned out to be middle aged or older. I thought, "This is very strange, I've never

read any fairy tales except about children or adolescents![1]"

Chinen went on to read many folk tales, and discovered a whole genre of "middle tales," which further broke down into two categories: tales where the protagonists were old, and tales where they were middle aged. A sub-set of the middle tales was specifically about men at midlife. They dealt mainly with the masculine, and not so much with women and the feminine. He talked about those tales in his book, *Beyond the Hero*.[2]

Chinen says middle tales show several stages. The first involves settling down in life, adjusting to the fact that you have to work, and that the magic and innocence of youth disappears. (The old tale of the Shoemaker and the Elves shows this pattern.) Another stage is to reverse gender roles, so that men come to terms with their feminine side, and women come to terms with their masculine side. Then they have to renegotiate their relationship (the story of the King and the Lute Player).

The third one is coming to terms with the dark side of life: with death, evil, tragedy, and the notion that we don't control everything. The young Hero assumes that with enough effort, or wit, or courage, he can do everything. At midlife, that is eliminated. People get sick. People die. Bad things happen to good people. The bible story of Job is a good example of this.

I have been an avid reader of folk tales for many years, even though I have not always understood their symbolic or metaphorical message. Through reading Chinen's books, and those of

---

[1] Chinen, Allan B.; *Once Upon A Midlife*; Jeremy P. Tarcher, New York, NY, 1992.
[2] Chinen, Allan B. Beyond the Hero: Classic Stories of Men in Search of Soul. Jeremy P. Tarcher; New York, NY, 1992.

Michael Meade as well as some others, I came to understand that what I was going through in "andropause", or my midlife transition, was normal, and had been going on for thousands of years. I suppose that is why I took up story telling. Aside from the entertainment value, folk tales may bring you insight into the highways you take in life, and some solace in that other men are riding the same "big slab."

Would You Rather Die Than Change?

If a well-informed trusted authority said you had to change your lifestyle - diet, exercise, mental approaches to stress - or you would die much sooner than necessary, would you change?

Before you say, "Of course!" think about this: if you are like nine out of ten people, you would find it so hard to adopt new habits that you would give up and die. Want proof?

About two million North Americans with heart disease have either bypass surgery or angioplasties every year. Their arteries usually clog up again within a few months to a few years unless they make some lifestyle changes. But 90% of the patients don't sustain the necessary changes in lifestyle.

At one time or another, you have probably tried to change yourself. Maybe you wanted to drop a bad habit, or develop a new way of reacting in stressful situations, or change the way you do business. Even harder, you may be in a supervisory position at work, and have to try to get other people to change.

Buying into Myths Prevents Change

Myth: Crisis is a big motivator of change.
Reality: Crisis may cause some short term adjustments, but it does not sustain long-term change.

Myth: Change is sustained by fear.
Reality: Fear is too hard to endure on a long-term basis, so we slip into denial and go back to our old ways. The crisis is passed and we hope it doesn't happen again.

Myth: The facts will convince us to change.
Reality: We really make decisions by stories and emotions. If the facts don't jibe with our view of the world, we reject them. "My mind is made up, don't confuse me with facts."

Myth: Small, gradual changes are easiest to sustain.
Reality: Big, sweeping changes are often easier; because we see benefits soon enough to get the positive reinforcement we need to keep going.

Myth: As we get older our brains won't accept changes (the "you can't teach an old dog new tricks" theory).
Reality: Brain research shows we can change at any age. The key is to continue learning new things, which keeps our brains flexible. When we want to make a real change, we have to 'carve a new neural pathway' in our brains.

The REAL keys to Change

In the early 1990s Dr. Dean Ornish, a professor of Medicine at the University of California designed a vegetarian-based diet he said could reverse heart disease without surgery or drugs. The medical establishment was sceptical, so Dr. Ornish persuaded Mutual of Omaha to fund a research trial. They put 333 patients with severely clogged arteries into a holistic program that included Dr. Ornish's diet, plus regular support groups meetings, and instruction in meditation, relaxation, yoga and aerobic exercise.

After three years, 77% of the patients were still 'doing the program', and had avoided angioplasties or bypasses. It saved Mutual of Omaha about $30,000 per patient. Here's why it worked:

- Ornish helped the patients get a positive picture of their future. Fear of death is not as strong a motivator as the pull of a desirable future.

- He made sweeping changes in their diets, which brought immediate results: 91% fewer chest pains in the first month. He says people who make moderate changes to their diet are worse off because they feel deprived, and don't see much change.

- He gave them wide-ranging help, from support groups to consultations with dieticians, psychologists, and yoga and meditation instructors.

Create New Neural Highways

Here's a tip from leading edge brain science: don't try to change. Create something new.

As you think your thoughts, and do your activities, your brain creates neural pathways. As you repeat activities or thoughts, these pathways become more like neural highways. You begin to have habitual ways of reacting in certain situations (such as blowing up at the people you supervise when things go wrong at work, or leaping in with "yes, but..." all the time when you are in a heated argument with your partner/spouse).

It is extremely difficult to change these neural pathways, but it is not difficult to start new ones.

Here is a simple example: Long ago, I used to smoke regularly. I decided to quit, but didn't have any real success. I would be at a party, and someone would offer me a cigarette. I would say,

"I'm quitting." But eventually I would decide I was not quitting just then, so would take the cigarette.

I was talking about this with a fellow one time, and he said, "You have it wrong in your mind. Instead of telling yourself you are quitting, which means every time you are offered a cigarette, you have a decision to make about whether to 'keep quitting', tell yourself, 'I don't smoke.' That way, there is no decision to make when someone offers you a cigarette."

I tried it, and it worked. I created a new non-smoker neural pathway in my brain. (I hasten to add that I still smoke cigars from time to time at men's conferences and while visiting my dad, but feel no urge to smoke regularly.)

The next time you are trying to change yourself, rather than wrestling with the old neural superhighway, head off across country and make a new path. It will be easier.

How to Change For the Better:
- Think about, and WRITE DOWN what you want in your life (the picture of a positive future that will help you change). And here is a secret: it will be more powerful, and easier to accomplish, if you include your wife and children in this exercise, having them ALL talk about what they would like their future to look like.
- Look at every aspect of your home and business life, and determine which conditions/activities are helping you get where you want to go, and which are just keeping you running on the spot. Drop the ones that aren't helping.
- Next, make a plan. You could use the "Life Time Goal Setting Exercise" from my website: www.AHarleyorMyWife.com - to help you allocate the

amount of time you will spend gaining balance and fulfilment in your life.

• Make a financial plan so that you know you have the
means to make the changes you desire.

Sound hard? It is - at first. But then maybe what you are doing now isn't all that easy either. And as the Chinese saying goes,
if you don't change direction, you'll end up where you're headed.

The Danger of Limiting Thoughts

I get quite a few emails from men saying they feel as though they
don't matter to anybody. If you feel a bit like that, here is a little
exercise that could maybe help you feel more valued. Chances
are pretty good that the people you are close to would be amazed
if they knew how you felt.

Let's say you think your family takes you for granted. All you
are is 'the old guy who brings home the money'. And let's also say
you don't think your boss appreciates your contribution to the
company (that is a fairly common feeling at midlife too). It's time
to sort yourself out using this helpful process:

You take a sheet of paper, and write the three column head-
ings, and then write the appropriate information under each
heading. It might look something like this:

BELIEF	EMOTION	BEHAVIOUR
My family takes me for granted	anger, resentment	angry outbursts, hurtful remarks, acting withdrawn and sullen
My boss doesn't appreciate my contribution to the company	resentment, anger, fear of being down sized	work is less creative and thorough than it could be

Now, look at what you wrote, and see whether:

- You need to rethink or adjust your beliefs (Is it really true your family takes you for granted? One way to find out would be to talk to them about it. They might be surprised.)
- You would benefit from getting a different perspective on the belief, so you could have a more positive, less stressful emotional reaction.
- You need to change a behaviour, even if it is based on a correct belief, and see whether that might create more fulfilling relationships.

Simply doing the exercise can give you valuable insights into what you believe and how you react to people. The first time I did an exercise like this, I was amazed at the amount of resentment, fear and anger I felt toward people close to me. Much of it was based on false assumptions (beliefs) I could discard. Even when my beliefs about others were correct, my relationship with them improved when I talked to the person involved and/or told a trusted friend how I felt. It gave me a great sense of freedom.

'isness' Lowers Stress

I knew a Cree elder who talked about 'isness', which is to say, things are as they are, and fighting that fact only causes stress.

Here's what I mean: Long ago I worked with native co-ops. My supervisor didn't believe the new co-ops I was helping to start would be successful, so he worked behind my back to prevent them from getting the funding they needed. He did not know that I knew what he was doing, so I was able to work behind his back in order to undo the work he did behind my back. Sick, eh?

I never did confront him on it, and eventually I quit that job. But while I was there, I obsessed about the guy. How he shouldn't do what he was doing. How he should work with me, and not try to hinder my projects. I burned up a lot of energy, and had a knot in my gut thinking about what a jerk this guy was, and how my life would be better if I had a different boss.

And that's where knowing about 'isness would have helped. The stress I was feeling was not due to the 'bad' supervisor. It was due to my story about how he should be different. But the reality was, he was *not* the way he *should* be. He was the way he *was.*

Since I learned about 'isness' a number of years ago, I monitor the stories I tell myself about how things should be, and in general have let them go when they do not jibe with how things are. I have less stress in my life because of it.

A few days ago I read *Loving What Is* by Byron Katie, co-written with Stephen Mitchell. Katie was in a deep depression in 1986, and had an "awakening" where she suddenly realized it was the stories she told herself about her life that were making her depressed. (I hasten to add that not all depression is caused by false stories. Some is clearly biochemical.) Anyway, Katie began to share her discovery with others, and many of those peoples' lives improved dramatically. She now gives workshops all over the world. She has developed, "Four questions that can change your life."

Katie has a website as well: www.thework.org. You can download a page with the four questions on it, and even some question forms, to use in your own life. But before doing that, I highly recommend you read the book, as it will give you a much clearer picture of how to use the questions.

I found the book very useful. I wish I would have read it years ago! It is, in some ways, a spiritual as well as practical book, as the great masters ALL emphasize the value of being in the moment, which is what this book helps one do.

Here is a very brief précis of her approach:

First, write down a limiting thought. Then ask the following four questions, writing down your answers. Do it slowly, really pondering before you give an answer:

1. **Is this thought true?** (Or is it just a thought you've become emotionally attached to?)

2. **(If yes, or not sure) Can I absolutely know that it's true?**

3. **How do I react when I think that thought?** Make a long list of your actions, behaviour, feelings and other thoughts that arise in the wake of the original thought.

4. **Who would I be without that thought?** If you are obsessing about how your boss doesn't appreciate you, how would your life be different if you were simply not able to think that thought?

Finally, turn the thought around. That is, state the limiting thought in reverse: "My boss does appreciate me." Or "I don't appreciate my boss", or even "I don't appreciate me." And then ask yourself if that new statement is just as true or truer than the original. You may be surprised by your answer.

One of the keys to letting go of limiting thoughts is to first recognize them! Here are some things to notice:

- **Limiting thoughts become like the air around us.** We take them for granted, thinking they are true. The more attached we are to them, and the more we defend them, the more likely they are limiting to us.
- **Limiting thoughts cause stress.** They are like an addiction: we think we will feel better thinking them (just as we think drinking will make us feel better), but in the end they don't.
- **We often blame others in our limiting thoughts.** We tell ourselves our lives would be better if only others would act differently, (treat us better, appreciate us more), and that we are powerless to do anything about it. Limiting thoughts contain words such as 'can't, impossible, should, shouldn't, always, never, and difficult.

So why not try this: identify one limiting thought, and use the 'Four Questions and Turnaround' on it. If you like the result, find another limiting thought and process it.

I have used this process myself a number of times, sometimes more than once on the same limiting thought (some limiting thoughts are persistent!), and have been pleased with the results. And that reminds me - I just thought of another limiting thought I think I will work on.

Playing the Stress Game

Some people hurry about, striding here and rushing there, always having too much to do, and making sure everyone knows it. This busyness can make a person seem important. (Gosh... he has ALL that to do! How does he get it all done?)

This rush through life can be a way to avoid intimacy as well. You can be "too busy" to take time for connecting deeply with spouse and/or family, so you don't have to risk the emotional discomfort that can accompany that kind of connection.

Stress can give you a bit of a 'rush,' too. When you are on the verge of overload and alarm, your body responds by pumping adrenaline into your system. You feel sharp and alert. Later of course, you crash, but that pumped-up feeling can be addictive. And don't forget that when you are stressed all the time, you live in a state of 'poor me,' and get sympathy from others.

If you're stress-addicted here's what you may be doing:

- You worry about all kinds of things you can't control.
- You procrastinate over taking action on the things you can control.
- When the situation looks really bad, you change a lot of things at once, so you can maintain a state of chaos.
- You 'work hard' all the time, no matter how you are feeling.
- You are a perfectionist in all you do, setting ridiculously high standards for yourself, and then beating yourself up for not meeting those standards.
- You don't exercise, and you watch lots of TV, or play computer games.
- You also make sure you eat whatever you want, including plenty of sugar, caffeine and maybe alcohol, so you put on weight, feel edgy, and don't sleep well.
- You avoid woo-woo practices that can bring inner peace, such as prayer and meditation.

- You suppress your sense of humour. Being stressed is serious business.
- You get rid of any social support system you have. You are a John Wayne clone, toughing it out, and suffering alone.
- You take everything personally, so you can be incensed over every little thing.

Maybe you are not the kind of person who thrives on being stressed all the time. In fact you want less stress. Try this:

- Accept that a certain amount of stress is good. When you have no stress, you are dead. The idea is to manage stress, not get rid of it.
- Exercise your funny bone. Laughter is a great way to keep stress in its place.
- Get serious about exercise. My research shows almost nothing is as effective as exercise for maintaining health, regulating weight, and fighting depression, which often goes hand-in-hand with stress.
- Manage your impulse spending. Follow my dad's advice: if you just have to have something, wait two weeks. If you still need it, go buy it. Put what you don't spend into savings, which can really help reduce financial stress.
- Be realistic about your expectations. A principle in Buddhism is that "frustration is caused by desiring that which will not be attained". Ergo - to avoid frustration, avoid desiring what you can't have.
- As the old song says, "keep on the sunny side". Much of what happens is out of your control, but how you react to it is 100% within your control.

- Maintain spiritual disciplines. Daily prayer and meditation, as well as belonging to a spiritual community can do much for inner peace and serenity.
- And perhaps most important: stay in touch with friends, spend time with family, give hugs with abandon, and let people know you love them. They'll do the same for you.

Why Does My Brain Quit Just When I Need It Most?

You know how it is... you get in a rip-roaring argument with your boss or your wife, and only when it's over do you think of what you SHOULD have said. As it was, you just reacted without thinking and came up with some genius expression such as "screw you."

When this happens to you, it never seems fair! You wonder why your brain quits just when you need it the most. Well, there is a chemical explanation, and it's even possible that long ago, the 'brain dead' syndrome was useful – even critical.

Here's the scoop. Stress affects the prefrontal cortex, the executive section of your brain that regulates thought, behaviour and emotion. New research suggests this happens through a messenger compound called protein kinase C (PKC). When you get stressed, your PKC production goes up, your creativity drops, and you can't remember stuff (like that whip-smart comeback to your boss you could have thought of if you weren't so riled).

When Amy Arnsten and her colleagues at Yale Medical School increased PKC levels in rats and monkeys, the animals got stupid. Before the test, they had an easy time finding a chocolate chip they had seen before. But after getting a chemical that increased their PKC levels, they had trouble finding it.

PKC may also be involved in bipolar disorder and schizo-
phrenia, as people suffering from both diseases appear to have
elevated PKC levels. Arnsten and her team are now working to
see whether blocking PKC production can help.

So what's the point of 'getting dumb' when you are under
stress? Some scientists think it is because it can be helpful to be
reactive under stress. When a saber-tooth is after you, your
primitive brain reacts by first sending the flight or fight response, and along with it a higher level of PKC. This happens
before your thinking brain (cerebral cortex) can stop and ponder
what the best course of action might be.

Okay, but what do you do in OUR WORLD when you are
stressed? When I was a TV news reporter facing a tight deadline
and my brain wouldn't cooperate, I would take a short break and
think about something else. When I returned to my keyboard,
even if only five minutes later, the words seemed to flow, and I
invariably met the deadline.

Maybe the best thing for you to do is to recognize how you
feel and work to calm down. Count to ten. Breathe deeply. Take a
break. Let your PKC level drop. And maybe you'll get your brain
back online!

Men and Depression

Approximately 40% of men in the forty to sixty midlife age
range will experience some degree of depression.

When I was going through my own andropause (midlife transition) I went through a period where I would suddenly feel
anxious and turn pale for about ten minutes twice a day - in mid-
morning, and mid-afternoon. This went on for about four
months. My wife, Elizabeth, would notice I was looking pale and

ask me if something was wrong. I would say I felt a bit anxious, but didn't know why.

I had what I now recognize as a low-grade depression (technically called Dysthymia) for several years. I thought I was just feeling kind of punk, and had lost interest in what I used to do. If I could find something new to be passionate about, I would feel fine. Elizabeth, who is a psychologist, helped me identify it as mild depression.

I never did see a doctor about this, but did mention it one time when I was having a regular medical. My doctor said if I ever wanted to just talk about stuff, I could come and see him. I said thanks, I'll think about it, but never did go see him just to talk. If I had wanted to see a professional for talk therapy I would have gone to a psychologist, (I have done that in the past), but I didn't do that either. I did not seek treatment for it, as it seemed an integral part of the process I was in. I did not consider it a health risk then. I know differently now.

Antidepressants

I didn't want to go on an anti-depressant, because I felt what I was going through was a normal part of life, and it would pass. Eventually it did, and I am still not sure whether an antidepressant would have been a better choice than 'toughing it out'. Had I been seriously depressed (as in when you can barely get out of bed in the morning), I would definitely have gone on a medication.

On the other hand, I have several friends my age who did go on anti-depressants for a year or two in their early fifties, and found it very helpful. One rancher friend said he felt cornered by external circumstances of all kinds. He couldn't even make a decision about what to do on the ranch. He said if he had two things to do in a given day, he couldn't figure out which to do first. He went on an anti-depressant and he felt mentally sharper than he had in many years.

Many of the men I talked to about their own midlife struggles mentioned symptoms similar to what I experienced. After going through a painful separation and divorce, one man wrote to me:

> I never thought I would feel better. I kept wondering, why can't I shake this? What is wrong with me? I am 56 years old. Get on with it."

> After experiencing depression, reading about it, joining a divorce support group and attending a divorce adjustment retreat, this man concluded, "What I went thru was not unlike anything other people have, and will [go through]. You can't go around, over or under it, you must go thru it, as difficult as it is, and it is best not to try to put it off. I learned you just have to let it take its course. I was so lonely at times, but called friends, locally and long distance, and talked to them, using up $20.00 7/11 phone cards. Just going to the mall or coffee shop to be around people was good for me. I got out, and saw there was life out there. I did resent people who were happy and didn't seem to have any cares, and especially couples. Being invited for supper, or over to people's places was so cathartic, just to be around people, and in a different setting. I hated to come home, but had to. I don't even have a pet..."

This man's depression was largely triggered by his separation. And as he says, you can't go around, over or under it. This kind of depression, attached to an event such as separation, will usually subside with the passage of time. However, if you find yourself in such a depression, do things along the lines of what he did, make yourself go out, and talk to your friends. Holing up makes things worse, and can lead to suicide.

Apparently women are twice as likely to suffer from depression as men, but men are much harder to diagnose, because women tend to look inward when something is wrong (what could be wrong with me?), and men tend to look outward (what is wrong with my wife, my boss, the world...?). It can take more than two years on average for a depressed man to be properly diagnosed because it doesn't occur to him he could be depressed or he denies it's possible. Often a man sees depression as a sign of weakness – things would be better if the people in his life just treated him 'right.'

If you are wondering whether you might have a bit of depression, here is some information about depression in men from a University of California website:

Symptoms of Depression include:
- Prolonged sadness or unexplained crying spells.
- Significant changes in appetite and sleep patterns.
- Irritability, anger, worry, agitation, anxiety.
- Pessimism, indifference.
- Loss of energy, persistent lethargy.
- Feelings of guilt, worthlessness.
- Inability to concentrate, indecisiveness.
- Inability to take pleasure in former interests, social withdrawal.
- Unexplained aches and pains.
- Recurring thoughts of death or suicide.
- Loss of interest and enjoyment in life.

- Pervasive "low mood."
- Decreased interest in sex.

Depression is described as, "A colourful world gone to black and white."

Experiencing five or more of the symptoms listed above for two weeks or longer indicates major depression. Experiencing several of the above symptoms in a less acute, but longer duration can indicate the presence of Dysthymia, a chronic, moderate type of depression in which people are able to continue functioning but experience frequent irritability and vulnerability to stress.

Recent research studies indicate that among the general population in the United States, 80% of those with symptoms of depression are not diagnosed and treated. I could not find statistics for Canada, but no doubt they are similar.

Additionally, new research indicates that depression is often experienced differently in men than in women and that among men, prolonged symptoms in the form of excessive anger, aggression, alcohol and substance use, working or eating excessively, and anti-social behaviour can all be indicators of depression.

Depression is common among men, and can have serious consequences. Professor Robert Goldney, from Adelaide University, is an international expert on suicide. In his private practice as a psychiatrist he treats plenty of middle-aged men. "It may sound simplistic, crass even," he says, "but this is the reality of it - depression, depression, depression. If you could get rid of all depression, you could eliminate 50 per cent of suicides." Goldney says part of the problem is that men aged 25 to 55 generally don't talk about their depression. They don't turn to a doctor or a counsellor for help. "In some ways, depression is not in the vocabulary of these men," he says.

The following information comes from an article on the Lakeland School District's website: http://web.lakeland272.org.

Risk factors commonly associated with depression include:

- Primary risk: suicide.

- Secondary risks: low functioning, poor interpersonal relationships, unhappiness, low productivity, and long-term self-esteem issues.

- Among men there is a connection between heart disease and depression. Men with depression are more than twice as likely to develop coronary heart disease as those who are not depressive.

- Symptoms of heart disease typically occur 15 years after the first episode of depression, suggesting that untreated, depression can have an insidious effect on general health not unlike that of unremitting stress.

- Men with depression have a 71% higher heart-disease risk, and are 2.34 times more likely to die of heart disease than their non-depressed counterparts.

Other facts about depression and men:

- Because many men grow up believing that depression is primarily a women's illness, and perhaps a sign of weakness, men are much less likely to admit to depression or to seek help for it than women.

- Men are not as likely to show the typical signs of depression either. They do not usually cry, show sadness, loss of will, or verbalize an intention to hurt themselves. As a result their depression is hidden from those caring friends, family, partner or associate who might insist they seek help. For this reason, according to unpublished Center for Disease Control reports, men in the U.S.A. are about four times more likely than women to kill themselves via suicide.

- Men who feel like they no longer "measure up", feel physically weaker, sense that their outlets for pleasure are reduced, or who have experienced a personal loss are at risk for depression.

- Men who experience the loss of a significant supportive relationship are also at serious risk for depression. This type of loss can be either a romantic relationship or, as is often the case, the loss of a father who has been particularly supportive of them throughout their life.

- Job loss is another trigger for depression, as is physical illness such as cancer, heart disease, and low thyroid function. The link among these that relate to the onset of depression is a feeling of loss in terms of earning potential, virility, strength, control, and self-definition. For example, of the 33,000 people who committed suicide in Japan in 1999, one half was unemployed.

- Age: suicide (the most extreme expression of depression) in men peaks in the 20s and again in the 60s and 70s. Whereas men complete 20% of all suicides in the U.S.A., the suicide rate triples in midlife men and increases seven times in men over age 65. With a history of depression, the risk of suicide increases substantially.

- Alcoholism, much more common in men than women, leads to suicide in 10% of affected people.

During the time I was in the deepest depths of the 'under-world' in my own midlife transition, I discovered that if I was talking to a friend my age and mentioned some of the symptoms I was experiencing, such as loss of energy, focus, libido, and even lack of interest in what I had been passionate about, as well as feeling more emotional in general, nine times out ten the friend would say, "Are you having that too? I thought I was the only one." We would then go on to talk about what we were struggling with, and we'd both end up feeling a little better, knowing we weren't alone.

I also started asking men in their sixties and seventies what their late forties and fifties were like, and many said they had a real struggle, including being depressed, but now they felt great. That gave me hope, knowing the stage I was in would end.

If you are depressed, do as I say, not as I did. Don't just see your doctor; go in for that "talk." Oh... and keep your life partner in the loop about how you are feeling too. It can make a really big difference in your relationship.

Recommended Reading: *I Don't Want To Talk About It: Overcoming the Secret Legacy of Male Depression* by Terrence Real. (Real is a psychologist who has worked with many depressed men. I found his case studies particularly interesting.)

Warning: Men are Better at Ending it All

No one seems to know what is causing the increase in suicide rates among middle aged men, but some experts suggest it may be related to increase use of all kinds of prescription drugs. As we are aging, we are using far more drugs, and because drugs are available over the Internet, many are self-medicating with some power-ful drugs in combinations that doctors would not recommend.

A couple of my university classmates committed suicide dur-ing their middle years. When I began doing research on men at midlife, I found suicide rates among middle-aged men are much higher than for women, and the rate is increasing. A five-year analysis of death rates released by the American Center for Disease Control and Prevention discovered that the suicide rate among 45-to-54-year-olds increased nearly 20 percent from 1999 to 2004, the latest year studied, far out pacing changes in nearly every other age group.

Women attempt suicide more frequently, but men are more effective. Four out of five actual suicides are men. Of the more than 32,000 people who committed suicide in 2004, nearly half - 14,607 - were 40 to 64 years old (6,906 of those were 45 to 54). The numbers for the two age groups that traditionally commit suicide at higher rates, seniors and teens were: 5,198 were over 65 and 2,434 were under 21 years old. Eighty percent of all suicides in the US are white, and 20% are non-white (Asian, Black, Latino).

Men who live in rural areas, especially less-populated areas, such as the West, are more likely to commit suicide, and the majority of suicides happen in the spring, although I don't know whether anyone knows why.

My first experience with suicide happened when I was in high school. The victim was Gunnar, a family friend, who was 38 at the time. The neighbours were shocked, but not surprised. During the previous year or so, Gunnar, who lived by himself, had been told by his doctor to quit drinking alcohol, cut down on coffee, and quit smoking. Everybody thought he really didn't have much to live for.

Gunnar had no social support system. He had always lived with his dad, who had died a couple of years earlier. Gunnar was quiet and shy and, as one neighbour said, "He talked a bit when he was drinking, but when he was sober he didn't even talk to himself."

My friend Jim was severely depressed and at risk of suicide a few years ago. He went to the doctor for help with insomnia, and his doctor recognized the danger signs. The first thing his doctor asked was whether he had any guns at home. When Jim said he did, the doctor told him to give them to a neighbour for safe keeping for a while.

Jim then went on an anti-depressant, and had a number of sessions with a psychiatrist. As he recovered, he became interested in helping other men at risk of suicide, and now he gives talks at company safety meetings. He tells men that if they, or a person they work with, begin to do substandard work, become uncharacteristically lackadaisical in their work habits, come to work late, and/or begin to drink more, perhaps stopping for a few drinks on the way home, they may be in danger. He says you are seeing your work mate during his best eight hours, and the rest of his day is likely to feel much worse to him.

Warning Signs

Suicide is rarely a spur of the moment decision. In the days and hours before people kill themselves, there are usually clues and warning signs. The strongest and most disturbing signs are verbal: "I can't go on." "Nothing matters anymore." or even, "I'm thinking of ending it all." Such remarks should always be taken seriously. Of course, in most cases these situations do not lead to suicide. But, generally, the more signs a person displays, the higher the risk of suicide.

Here is some information regarding suicide that can be found on a number of websites:

Situations
- Suffering a major loss or life change
- Family history of suicide or violence
- Sexual or physical abuse
- Death of a close friend or family member
- Divorce or separation, ending a relationship
- Failing academic performance, impending exams, exam results
- Job loss, problems at work
- Impending legal action
- Recent imprisonment or upcoming release

Behaviours
- Showing a marked change in behaviour, attitudes or appearance
- Crying
- Fighting
- Behaving recklessly
- Breaking the law
- Impulsiveness
- Abusing drugs or alcohol
- Self-mutilation
- Writing about death and suicide
- Previous suicidal behaviour
- Extremes of behaviour

- Changes in behaviour
- Getting affairs in order and giving away valued possessions

Physical Changes
- Lack of energy
- Disturbed sleep patterns – sleeping too much or too little
- Loss of appetite
- Becoming depressed or withdrawn
- Sudden weight gain or loss
- Increase in minor illnesses
- Change of sexual interest
- Sudden change in appearance
- Lack of interest in appearance

Thoughts and Emotions
- Thoughts of suicide
- Loneliness – lack of support from family and friends
- Rejection, feeling marginalized
- Deep sadness or guilt
- Unable to see beyond a narrow focus
- Daydreaming
- Anxiety and stress
- Helplessness
- Loss of self-worth

Helping someone who is suicidal

Here is some advice from an Australian website called Suicide Help Line:

> Letting them express their thoughts and feelings can help a suicidal person "share the load" of their troubles and put things in perspective. It's important not to minimise their problems or be judgmental. Avoid statements such as, "You don't know how lucky you are." And, "You shouldn't feel like that." Instead, acknowledge the pain they're experiencing right now. Often, knowing someone cares enough to get involved and listen can be a great help to someone who is suicidal.

> Supporting someone who is suicidal can be exceptionally hard on you and it's important that you also look after yourself. It might be beneficial to seek professional support yourself, or to talk about things to someone close to you.

There is a lot more helpful information on this website that I recommend if you think someone you know might be suicidal. We are at a dangerous age, but we can get through it by acting as the 'crash padding' for each other.

Midlife Burnout

One of the most common statements I hear from middle-aged men is that they feel burned out, and unappreciated. They feel as though all they do is work, while their wives and kids spend the money, and want more. Nobody even says thank you. They just expect the old man will keep on putting out. It makes them dream of kicking over the traces and taking off, maybe on a

Harley with a high-breasted young maiden behind who will appreciate them – not to mention being almost continuously aroused!

While it may be true that many men's families don't express much appreciation for the work they do and the money they make, I think a part of this feeling of dissatisfaction is due to what might be called midlife burnout.

You may start to wonder what life is really all about. You might feel you need a sabbatical, desperately want to take time to think about things for a while and rest. Instead your load is actually getting heavier.

By the time you reach midlife, you have a lot of skills and experiences, and people in every part of your life - at work, at home, at organizations you belong to, want to take advantage of them. They ask you to take on more commitments. And being a good guy, you usually do.

At the same time, you have less physical stamina than you used to have. In your twenties and even thirties, you recovered more quickly than you do in your forties and beyond. For example, three years ago I cracked a couple of ribs when a horse bucked me off. I asked my son-in-law, a medical doctor, how long it would take to heal. He said about 6-8 weeks. Probably true for a younger person, but I was 57 at the time, and it took almost a year!

You may also find you can't handle stress quite as well. Again because you don't have the physical resiliency you used to have. This adds to the extra load you are carrying. Maybe that's one reason you feel more irritable at midlife!

Another question that starts jabbing you around age 35-45 is what I call the "right livelihood" question, "What is my true vocation?" At 17, you decided you would be an accountant, a dentist, a mechanic, whatever, maybe because there was supposed to be good money in it. Now it isn't feeding your soul, and you feel as though you are missing your true work, even though you don't quite know what that is. A 47-year-old man emailed me to say he is a church minister, and is no longer finding the work rewarding; but does not know what will spark his passion anew.

This can be a stressful time. That's why it is called midlife burnout. In my 50s I wondered whether the loss of energy, libido, focus, and confidence would ever end. But here is the good news: as with all things, this too shall pass. You need to do a certain amount of self-care - maybe get a personal/professional coach to help you clarify your true vocation, talk to your wife about feeling taken for granted. Maybe she truly appreciates you, but forgot to mention it. By the way... it is good to express appreciation for her contribution too.

Good diet, enough sleep, and some regular physical exercise can go a long way toward reducing your stress as well; and getting together with friends can also be a true balm when feeling burned out. I adopted these practices and have the energy back I had in my forties, but I feel calmer and more relaxed. Little things don't get to me any more, and I am nowhere near as irritable!

A Time of Ashes

There comes a time (or times) in everyone's life when calamity hits - you are downsized, divorced, in a car accident, a close family member dies, you lose your business, or lose interest in your work, or some other catastrophe comes along. Our old world falls away, and we don't know what will take its place. It is called a "Time of Ashes".

We all know stories of a time of ashes. In the Bible, the story of Job, who was wealthy and happy, is perhaps the best example. His life is going along fine: wealth, lovely family, lots of stuff. Then it is all taken away, and his life is grim. He stays true to the spiritual path and eventually he gets it all back.

I, and no doubt you, have been in similar situations, although maybe not as dramatic, where things fall away, and nothing I try seems to work. For me, the latest 'time of ashes' started in 1997 when Elizabeth and I moved to Vancouver. The idea was for me to join the management team of a start-up company we had invested in.

But it was as though some giant invisible hand was holding everything back. Every time we found a major investor for the company, something would happen just before they invested. Some potential investors went bankrupt, one went to jail, and one had a personal breakdown. It was as though our company was the 'kiss of death' for anyone who tried to invest with us. Eventually we gave up.

At the same time, I lost energy, focus, confidence and passion, and could not seem to get anything else started. I tried everything from public speaking to network marketing, but couldn't get anything off the ground. I slowly came to realize I was going through some kind of transformation at a very deep level, but could not wilfully bring the process into consciousness. I just had to trust that the right thing was happening, and at some point, it would end.

In the meantime, our retirement savings were disappearing at an alarming rate, and there didn't seem to be anything we could do about it. This 'paralysis' lasted for several years.

I have met others who have had harder struggles, such as a woman in Vancouver who at age 50 lost her job as a corporate executive, lost her husband, became mentally ill, and eventually ended up living on the streets. After a few years she 'rose out of the ashes,' and when I met her, she was an artist, living in a small apartment. She had cobbled together a life more fulfilling than the career and marriage she had lost.

If you are in a 'time of ashes,' stay the course, explore in whatever way you can what is trying to be called forth, and know that this is a normal part of midlife, and this too shall pass. As with Job, we usually recover lost ground financially as well, which I am happy to report, Elizabeth and I have done.

The good thing about a time of ashes is that it is also the beginning of a fuller understanding of life. It helps you become more compassionate and openhearted, and less judgmental, as you know what it is like to fail or to experience pain. It also leads you in the direction of your soul's calling.

Ride the Road

The Power of "I statements"

You know how it feels... somebody gets mad at you, and starts pointing fingers and telling you what you *should* or *shouldn't* have done. Or he tells you what a jerk you are for forgetting something. Or she points out what a cad you are for not noticing something (such as a new hairdo). No doubt you have done the same to someone else, especially your children. After all, you learned it from *your* parents.

If you have ever noticed your reaction when somebody is *shoulding* on you, you know you stop hearing what they are saying long before they are done talking. You are waiting for an

opening so you can "Yes, but ..." them... "Yes, but you forgot to
_____." or "Yes, but you always _____." The
conversation goes downhill from there. The reason is you are
using "You" statements. As in "You forgot _____," or
"You always _____," or "You never _____," or
"You don't care _____."

If you want to stop those go-nowhere shouting matches before
everybody ends up feeling angry and defensive, use "I" statements.
Here's how it works: let's say your wife has done something to
upset you. Maybe she wrote a big cheque on the joint account and
forgot to tell you, so one of your cheques bounced. Your inclina-
tion might be to tear into her: "Darn it Martha, how many times do
I have to tell you to let me know when you write a big cheque?
Don't you ever think?" And on and on.

Martha's only logical response is to get behind the barricades
and start shooting "yes buts" back at you: "Yes, but how about a
couple of weeks ago when I went to pay for the groceries with
my debit card and found there was no money in the account?
What about that, mister perfect?"

And back and forth you go, hurling accusations and counter-
accusations, until you give up out of sheer weariness, and one of
you is sleeping on the couch.

But let's take the same scenario, and use "I" statements:"

You: "Martha, I wrote a cheque for some new golf clubs a
couple of days ago, and the guy at the store phoned today
to say the cheque had bounced. I felt like a fool. When I
checked the account, I found out you wrote a big cheque
last Tuesday and didn't tell me about it. I hate it when a
cheque of mine bounces. I think people must see me as

some kind of loser. And I'm angry that you didn't tell me about that big cheque."

Now, notice that everything you said started with "I:" I wrote a cheque, I felt like a fool, I am angry, and so on. You have stuck to the facts about what happened and how you feel about it, and not once pointed the finger at Martha and called her names.

Martha is understandably nervous about your anger, but because you haven't pointed fingers and said what a fool she is, she doesn't have to get behind the barricades to defend herself.

She can now say something such as: "I'm sorry Frank. I meant to tell you on Tuesday, but then Sally didn't come to work, and I had to cover for her, and the boss was mad, and by the time I got home after four hours of overtime, I guess I forgot. I know how it feels to have a cheque bounce, and I am truly sorry. If there is anything I can do to make up for it, I will."

Now, the conversation may go back and forth a little more from there, such as talking about how you can avoid bounced cheques in the future, but essentially the problem is solved and you both might feel like a little lovin' tonight!

You see how that works? Just stick with the facts:
- This is what I think happened
- This is what I think it means
- This is how I feel about it

What on Earth am I Feeling?

One of my coaching clients complained that his wife always wanted to know what he felt. "When I tell her I'm not feeling anything," he said, "she gets mad and thinks I'm withholding." I have heard this complaint from men many times, and used to experience it myself.

As I worked with this man, he began to realize he actually did have lots of feelings, but he either didn't know what they were, or he didn't want to admit them to her (for example, he didn't like admitting he resented something she had done because it seemed "too small.")

Possibly you, like the majority of men, have been socialized from the time you were a wee lad to discount your feelings. In fact it seems men are only allowed four feelings: anger, lust, feeling good, and love (often another name for lust). Your feelings are often buried in a bone yard of spare parts under a life's worth collection of other parts.

I developed a process that worked for me and will help you dig your feelings out of that bone yard. Try it. You might find it works for you. After a while, you do it automatically.

1. Learn to pay attention to your gut, especially when you are in an emotional situation such as an argument or some other conflict.
2. When you get a hit in your solar plexus area (where emotions reside), think to yourself, 'uh-oh, I'm having a feeling.'
3. Recognize you are getting it, even if you can't identify the feeling.
4. Think, 'what is a logical way to feel under these circumstances?' (e.g., anger, sadness, resentment etc.)
5. When you come up with what seems a logical feeling to your mind, check in with your gut to see if that is what you are, in fact, feeling. Often you are correct.
6. Tell the person with whom you are in conflict what you feel, and what it is about the situation that makes you feel that way. This is, for some, the hardest part of the process,

but often the most valuable and rewarding. For instance, if the conflict is with your partner, and you take the time to work out your feelings and explain, your partner sees you in a more sympathetic/loving light. Often, this means spontaneous sex and a warmer relationship.

Next time your wife wants to know what you are feeling about a situation, just say, "Hang on honey, let me go inside and check." Then go through the process. You might be surprised by what you find. And your wife will be happy when you tell her.

SECTION TWO

Under the Paint is a Great Body

For a Healthy Heart, Dump the Grump

It is fairly common for men in midlife to become irritable. If you get stuck in this "irritable" gear, you become a "grumpy old man," and stay mad at the world – you are at risk for a stroke or heart attack.

A study published in the *Journal of the American Heart Association* in March, 2004, found that certain measures of anger and hostility are related to the development of atrial fibrillation in men.

Atrial fibrillation is an irregular heart rhythm (arrhythmia) in which the two upper chambers of the heart quiver instead of beating effectively. This means these chambers aren't completely emptied when the heart beats, so blood can pool and form clots, which can cause a stroke. It affects about 2 million Americans and is increasing as the population ages.

The study carried out by Elaine D. Eaker, of Eaker Epidemiology Enterprises, LLC, in Chili, Wisconsin, in cooperation with colleagues at Boston University and the Framingham Heart Study, included 1,769 men and 1,913 women. They completed psychological surveys when their average age was 48.5 years and they had no signs of heart disease. They were followed for 10 years.

The researchers found that men with more feelings of hostility were 30 percent more likely to develop atrial fibrillation than men with lower hostility levels. Hostility, as measured by the Minnesota Multiphasic Personality Inventory, is a general feeling of contempt toward other people. Hostile people expect the worst from others and agree with statements such as:

- "I have often met people who were supposed to be experts who were no better than me."
- "I frequently have worked under people who arrange things so they get all the credit."
- "Some of my family members have habits that bother me and annoy me very much."

Men who scored high in trait-anger ('disposition to experience anger') had a 10 percent greater risk of developing atrial fibrillation than men who didn't go around mad all the time. The men with high trait-anger scores described themselves as fiery, or quick-tempered, hot-headed, annoyed when slighted, furious when criticized, and wanting to hit someone when frustrated. These men were also 20 percent more likely to have died from any cause during the ten years of the study.

Men also had a 20 percent higher risk of developing atrial fibrillation if they rated high in "symptoms of anger," such as shaking, headaches, and muscle tension.

Dump the Grump

If this is sounding all too familiar, and you identify yourself as heading for "grumpy old men" territory, I suggest you try some of the things that helped me gear back my irritability when I went through this phase. You may save your life if you:

- Pay a lot of attention to your spiritual growth, seeking a deeper connection with the Creator
- Spend a bit of time and effort discerning your "right" livelihood, so you do the work that fulfills you.
- Keep your marriage/relationships strong, treating those you love with kindness and patience, especially when one or the other, or some times both of you, are feeling particularly stressed.
- It can also be useful to see a psychotherapist to help you work out any life issues you can't seem to manage on your own. I have done that more than once, always with good results.

Your Libido Is Changing, and That's OK

The 50s are the next best thing to the 20s in the bedroom

Approximately four hundred men filled in the sexual life questionnaire I had on my website a few years ago. Here are some results:

- 43.4% said, "I have lower libido than a few years ago, but still enjoy sex with my wife/partner."

- 37.3% said, "I have a lower sex drive than I used to have, but I still would like more sex than my wife/partner is interested in."
- 41.7% said, "I am not enjoying sex with my wife/partner as much as I used to, but fantasize about having sex with younger women."
- 36.3% said they were having an affair, either for the great sex, or for companionship.
- 20% are taking a medication that is either affecting their sexual functioning, or reducing their desire.
- 20% are taking a medication to improve the strength of their erections.

The ages of the men were:
- 7% were 35-40 years
- 50% were 40-50 years
- 36% were 50-60 years
- 7% were 60 years or older

I am not able to break these responses down into answers by age category. Most men selected more than one answer, often selecting both. For example: "I have a lower sex drive than I used to have, but I still would like more sex than my wife/partner is interested in," and, "I am not enjoying sex with my wife/partner as much as I used to, but fantasize about having sex with younger women."

A study published in Norway, and reported in the CanWest news service stated that a study by researchers at the University of Oslo, University of Bergen and Harvard Medical School, says men in their 50s have the highest level of satisfaction with their sex life since their 20s. Even more than men in their 30s and 40s.

The study surveyed nearly 1200 men in Norway, and found that although men in their 50s are losing a bit of physical oomph, they enjoy sex more than they did during their younger years because they don't have the same performance hang-ups younger men have.

It all makes perfect sense to Guy Grenier, a psychologist and sex therapist who teaches at the University of Western Ontario. "In older age groups, people are less hung up about performance," he says. "These results are consistent with what we find in women as well. People have learned more about themselves. They are more comfortable in their relationships. They have found ways to express their sexual needs. They're more focused on commitment and attachment, so sex becomes ...a moment to be intimate and to bond with somebody."

What Grenier says rings true in my own experience. Although I have a lower libido than a few years ago, and Elizabeth does too, we find our bedroom encounters are more intimate and satisfying.

Now here is the not-so-good part: the study found that satisfaction dropped off sharply for men in their 60s and beyond.

OOPs – Erectile Dysfunction

Risk for heart disease now, may increase risk for erectile dysfunction later

A study reported in the *Journal of the American College of Cardiology* shows that obesity, high cholesterol, and high triglyceride measurements in midlife, which are known to be predictors of heart disease, also predict the likelihood of erectile dysfunction decades later.

Back in the early seventies, 1810 men from Rancho Bernardo, California participated in a survey of coronary heart disease risk factors. The participants, aged 30 to 69 at the time, had a brief medical, had their medication history taken, and were measured for height, weight, blood pressure, fasting plasma glucose, cholesterol, and triglyceride levels. Twenty five years later, in 1998, a survey was sent to the 944 men who were still living. Of those, 570 surveys were returned with complete answers to questions about erectile function. They discovered:

- Mean age, body mass index, cholesterol, and triglycerides were each significantly associated with an increased risk of erectile dysfunction.

- Cigarette smoking was marginally more common in those with severe or complete erectile dysfunction, as compared with those without. Blood pressure and fasting blood glucose were not significantly associated with erectile dysfunction. The authors wrote that the lack of association was probably due to higher death rates among men with higher blood pressure or blood sugar levels. (Almost all of the surviving men either had never smoked, or had quit smoking.)

So... if you are middle-aged and overweight, have high cholesterol and/or high triglyceride measurements (you can find those out from blood tests), you not only risk a heart attack any day, but when you get older, you may also have problems "getting it up".

An approach you may find useful in controlling your weight (which goes a long way to controlling the other symptoms) is following Dr. Barry Sear's advice for balanced eating from his book *Mastering the Zone.* I lost 20 pounds and dropped my cholesterol by 50% in five months several years ago, without experiencing any excessive hunger or cravings. Also see his website: http://www.zonediet.com/

I don't know about you, but I am interested in living a long HEALTHY life, and I see no reason to give up sex just because I reach my 70s!

Chowin' Down – Sausage versus Cereal

When I want a snack, I want some meat. I don't want any puny little veggies or fruits. Sausage is always appealing, or some kind of cold cut. It turns out I am a pretty typical male.

A study reported in the latest issue of *The Journal Of Men's Health And Gender*(Volume 2, Issue 2, June 2005, Pages 194-201) says women eat more fruits, vegetables, cereals, milk and other dairy products and whole grain products, and men lean toward red meat, as well as pork, sausages, eggs, alcohol, and starchy foods such as potatoes and bread.

When it comes to sweet foods, men and women are about the same. The favourites of course are chocolate, ice cream, cakes, cookies and wafers.

Apparently the reasons for these differences in eating preferences are psychological and socio-cultural. In our society it is more acceptable for men to be a bit overweight than for women, so women try harder not to gain weight. They know more about nutrition than men, and are more likely to practice "restrained eating" (not eating as much as they would like). Society also views fruits and vegetables more as feminine foods, and meat (representing strength and virility) as masculine food.

Men generally eat for pleasure, and are not all that concerned about the nutritional value of what they eat. Women are more influenced by social norms in what they eat. They are generally less satisfied with their weight than men are, and are more likely to think they weigh more than they actually do. Men typically underestimate how much they weigh.

As far as health goes, men count on sports and exercise to stay healthy, whereas women depend more on diet and nutrition. In spite of being more nutritionally aware, and eating 'healthier foods' (at least that's the way women see their food choices), the number of overweight men and women is about the same.

Men Are Apples, Women Are Pears

When it comes to being overweight, men tend to put it on around the middle - the stomach and organs. This is called visceral fat, so overweight men are shaped more like apples. Women accumulate fat around the hips and butt, and are shaped more like pears. The bad news is that it is more dangerous to be an apple than a pear. The good news is that it is easier to lose visceral fat than 'gynoid fat' (the kind women put on).

Either way, there are many advantages to losing weight. For example, losing 10 Kg. (a little more than twenty pounds):

- reduces total mortality (chances of dying) by more than 20%
- reduces triglycerides (you don't want these accumulating in your blood) by more than 30%
- reduces LDL (bad) cholesterol by 15%
- increases HDL (good) cholesterol by 8%
- lowers blood pressure
- improves lung function
- reduces back pain

So there you go. Men don't eat right, but enjoy it more, and are no fatter overall than women.

The Danger of Genetically Modified Organisms (GMOs)

I was a television news reporter with the Canadian Broadcasting Corporation back in the late 70s when genetic engineering came on the scene. I have a couple of degrees in agriculture, and from what I was learning from the scientists I talked to, genetic engineering held out a lot of promise. We could grow foods with higher protein content, create grains that would grow in saline soils, maybe even develop grain crops that could fix their own nitrogen, and farmers would not have to use as much chemical fertilizer.

Of course none of that promising technology was ever developed. The major corporations that took over the genetic engineering industry spend most of their effort on developing crops that can withstand pesticides, or that have their own built-in pesticides.

But the scientists back then believed, as did all genetic engineers at the time, that taking a gene from one life form and putting it into another was a clean, simple process. What could go wrong?

Well... in a word, lots.

Over the years I talked to various biotech scientists who were becoming worried about whether the genetically-modified foods entering the food chain were safe. As the science developed, it was discovered the process of genetic engineering is anything but straightforward. Chunks of genetic material jump all over the place once they are inserted into plants, and there is no predicting where they will go, or what effect they will have. There has been almost no research on the safety of genetically-modified foods, and what little has been done has shown these foods can cause a number of health problems ranging from allergies to food intolerances to cancer.

There is particular danger to babies and small children. (That includes our grandchildren.)

Both Canadian and US government agencies have taken the position (urged on by the biotech companies) that these new food crops are "substantially equivalent" to existing crops, so do not need to be studied for food safety. And both governments are strong supporters of the industry, just as I used to be.

A few years ago I became worried enough about the safety of these foods to make a serious effort not to eat any, or at least as few as possible (they are hard to avoid unless you buy organic food, as GMOs are in almost every kind of additive these days).

Reading *Seeds of Deception* by Jeffrey M. Smith raised my concern further. Men might not be the sole "provider" anymore, but we still bear the heavier part of the role "protector". It's not just the visible from which we need to protect our loved ones; the invisible can be just as dangerous.

I highly recommend this book: Smith, Jeffrey M.; *Seeds of Deception: Exposing Industry and Government Lies About the Safety of the Genetically Engineered Foods You're Eating;* Yes! Books; Fairfield, IA; 2003.

What's That? I Can't Hear You

I wear hearing aids. I got them a few years ago. Now people (especially my grandchildren) don't mumble half as much as they used to!

I got hearing aids because when I was young, invincible, and working on the farm and in the oil fields, I was too tough to use hearing protection. Only wimps wore safety stuff. Now I wish I had have been a little more careful.

A while back I read an article saying that 25% of the people who listen to MP3 players such as iPods are in danger of causing permanent hearing damage because they have the volume turned too high. Any sound above 90 decibels (db) could cause some hearing loss if the exposure is prolonged. Most portable music players can produce sounds up to 120 db, which is louder than a Harley (111 db at highway speed), a lawn mower or a chain saw and equivalent to an ambulance siren. The problem is that MP3 player headsets can be turned up loud without distorting the sound the way the headsets in the old Walkmans did. But they don't drown out background noise, so people turn them up. And because the sound is still good, they tend to listen longer.

According to the Mayo Clinic's website, your MP3 player is too loud if:

- Your MP3 player volume is set higher than 60 percent of the maximum
- You can't hear conversations going on around you
- People near you can hear your music
- You find yourself shouting instead of talking when you respond to people nearby

Noise Cancelling Headphones

I am reading more and more these days about the benefits of noise-cancelling headphones. The idea is that these headphones read the background noise, and produce the exact opposite sound waves, so the background sound is cancelled. "These headphones work most efficiently and effectively if you're in an environment that has that low-frequency steady state noise," says Pam Mason, MEd, director of the *Audiology Professional Practices Unit for the American Speech-Language-Hearing Association (ASHA).* This can be a boon for commuters, frequent flyers and city dwellers, who are exposed to the constant low frequency rumble of traffic, jet engines, Harley roar or tire noise. But they don't block everything. "You'll still hear that baby crying two rows back," Mason says.

Most noise-cancelling headphones allow you to attach an MP3 player, but they still protect your hearing because you don't need to turn the player up to overcome background noise. There are other, substantial health benefits as well.

"Noise is a stressor," explains Mason. "It can increase gastric secretions in your stomach and disrupt sleep and elevate blood pressure. So if you reduce the noise, you can reduce those negative effects."

Jodi Cook, Ph.D., director of the hearing aid program at Mayo Clinic, says you don't need one of these expensive headsets if you keep the volume on your normal headset at a level where you can still comfortably carry on a conversation. And you won't need to limit the amount of time you listen to your music either. You can listen at 80 db forever and never hurt your hearing.

A Quick Test to Check Your Hearing

I had known for a long time that I had some hearing loss. In 1987 I took a test that told me so. However, I waited a long time to get hearing aids, partly because my hearing "wasn't that bad yet," and partly because of the expense. You have probably noticed you are having a harder time following conversations in noisy restaurants or loud parties. If you would like to do a quick check of how your hearing in those circumstances compares with other people your age, check this out: http://bfc.positscience.com/eval/snr.php. If you do particularly poorly compared to your peers, you might want to go to an audio clinic and get a formal hearing test.

Covering the Cost

Workers Compensation looked after the expense for my hearing aids. In Alberta, if you have ever worked in a very loud environment, and can have your claim verified by someone else who also worked in that environment, Workers Compensation will pay $2500 toward hearing aids every five years, plus pay for your batteries for life. Coverage varies in other states and provinces. If you live in the USA or Canada, find out the coverage you are eligible for by going here: http://esion.com/workerscomp.pdf. In other countries, check your workers compensation website, or call their office.

So playing it cool has a down side – hearing loss. Maybe you didn't protect your hearing either, but then again, maybe you didn't work in a loud place when you were young, but play your MP3 player too loudly now. If so, turn it down. It takes quite a while for hearing loss to show up, but when it does, it's permanent. And believe me; it is better to have good hearing than to wear hearing aids.

Snoring

Several months ago, I started snoring more, and louder. During most of my life, I have snored when I have been over-tired, or back in my drinking days, when I had "'a bit too much".

My snoring is a problem in a number of ways:

• it makes it difficult for my wife to sleep
• it wakes me up at times, and I often have a dry throat, from open-mouthed snoring
• my research tells me it can be hard on my health

I missed a whole month of exercise class one December while the gym was undergoing annual maintenance, which coincided with the Christmas holidays, also known as "eating season." The result was I put on about nine extra pounds. I still haven't lost it all!

I started snoring more at about that time.

This little excerpt from the National Sleep Foundation website might explain why:

> Snoring is the primary cause of sleep disruption for approximately 90 million American adults; 37 million on a regular basis. Snoring is most commonly associated with persons who are overweight and the condition often becomes worse with age. Loud snoring is particularly serious as it can be a symptom of sleep apnoea and associated with high blood pressure and other health problems. In sleep apnoea, breathing stops – sometimes for as long as 10-60 seconds – and the amount of oxygen in the blood drops, often to very low. This alerts the brain, causing a brief arousal (awakening) and breathing resumes. These stoppages of breathing can occur

repeatedly, causing multiple sleep disruptions throughout the night and result in excessive daytime sleepiness
and impaired daytime function.

I was getting to the point where my sleep was significantly
interrupted with my snoring, and I even developed some apnoea.
I was starting to feel tired all the time.

I bought a little nose insert - a U-shaped piece of plastic I put
in my nose at bedtime, that holds my nostrils open, so I don't
breathe through my mouth so much. It helped some, but not
enough.

I have tried other devices to reduce snoring, including a
'Sleep Wizard' – a band you put over the top of your head and
under your jaw to keep your mouth closed while you sleep - but
haven't found anything that works all that well. I am committed
to losing those added ten pounds, as I think that is the best way
to stop, or at least reduce, snoring.

Down to the Short Strokes

Remember all those stories you heard when you were a kid
about going blind, or growing hair on the palms of your hands if
you masturbated? Of course you know now they are not true. But
wouldn't you have felt better back then if you knew what you
were doing might be reducing your risk of prostate cancer thirty
or forty years down the road?

In the July, 2003 issue of the scientific journal *BJU International (Volume 92 Issue 3, Pages 211 – 216)*, Australian scientists
published the results of a study of the sexual habits of more than
2300 men, roughly half of whom had been diagnosed with
prostate cancer. They found that the men who had frequent
ejaculations between the ages of 20 and 50 had a lower rate of

prostate cancer. And it didn't matter whether they had sex partners or not. Masturbation was just as effective as the real thing. This was especially true for men who had ejaculated at least five times a week during their 20s. Those men were one-third less likely to develop aggressive prostate cancer later in life.

According to Dr. Andrew Weil, M.D., "Masturbation is a normal expression of sexuality, and it's harmless unless you masturbate compulsively or cause yourself physical irritation. If this study's findings are confirmed, they should become part of the advice that doctors give men for protecting their reproductive systems."

If sex with your partner isn't as exciting as it used to be, and you find yourself daydreaming about having sex with other women, and are maybe masturbating more, and finding it more satisfying because you don't have to worry about not performing well, it has an upside. You are probably helping to keep your prostate healthy.

Talk Out Loud

The Life We Are Given: A Long-Term Program for Realizing the Potential of Body, Mind, Heart, and Soul by George Leonard and Michael Murphy has an exercise called "Taking the Hit as a Gift." They write, "Unexpected blows come in many varieties, from the merely bothersome to the profound... Our most common responses to such unfortunate happenings tend to make things worse."

What they mean is you usually react to the unexpected by reflex, and either fight back, or whine and snivel in a victim's way, or maybe you simply deny you felt anything, which puts you in the habit of not even knowing you are feeling anything. When I was a teenager, I thought it was cool to not react when some jerk tried to spook me by sneaking up behind and whacking me, or maybe giving a loud shout. I got good at it, and eventually almost nothing would make me flinch. When I got older and it turned out experiencing my feelings was actually a good thing, it took me quite a while to tune back in.

George Leonard, who is an Aikido master, suggests the kind of response cultivated in martial arts: fully experience and acknowledge the strong feelings, and use the energy to handle the situation.

To do the exercise, you need a partner. One person takes a balanced and centred stance, with the feet about shoulder width apart, and an arm out at a 45 degree angle. The other person sneaks up behind, and without warning, gives a loud shout, and simultaneously grabs and holds the arm, without pulling the person off balance.

If you're the person who is surprised, you should, Leonard says:

> ...be totally aware of how the sudden hit affected you. Speaking aloud in a clear voice, describe exactly what is going on within you. Specify exactly where in your body each feeling or sensation is located. Don't look at your partner as you speak. Resist the temptation to point the finger of your free hand at different parts of your body. Use words only, and be as specific as possible. For example: 'When you grabbed me, I jumped and blinked both eyes. My heart seemed to jump up into my throat. Now my throat feels a little dry. I can feel the pressure of your hands on my right wrist...'"

As you keep speaking, you'll notice that the conditions you describe seem to melt away. "Many people discover that merely becoming aware of an imbalance tends to correct it," Leonard says.

The second part of this exercise is to notice that the sudden hit has added energy to your body and mind. Your whole nervous system becomes more alert, and you can use the energy for whatever positive purpose you choose. (A normal reflex is to use the extra energy to fight back, but now, having this new knowledge, you can use it for something useful, such as working on a project you have been putting off.)

Leonard suggests you "take a series of deep breaths, move up and down rhythmically by bending and unbending your knees... ask your partner to release your wrist, and walk around the room expansively, arms open."

Talk It Out – Loud

When I read this exercise, I didn't have anybody handy to get to sneak up and scare me, so I decided to put the principle of speaking aloud about an anxiety I was feeling.

I had a new project coming up that I had not done before, and I was having some of the typical fears I get under such circumstances: "What if I can't do it right? "What if I don't know how?" "What if I fail miserably and nobody ever wants to hire me again?" I hasten to add that I was totally qualified, and knew I could do the job well, but some "chicken little" part always seems to get its voice in there just the same.

I decided to tune into my body where I was feeling this anxiety, and speak the fear out loud. "I feel some tension in my solar plexus area, and the fear is that I will not have sufficient skill to do the project properly. I feel a bit of tension in my shoulders, and the fear is that I will appear to be a fool." I continued with this exercise with my eyes closed in order to tune into my body as much as possible. Wherever I felt any kind of tension, I explored it, discovered what it was about, and spoke it out loud (needless to say, nobody was in the house to observe).

In a short time, all my anxiety about the project disappeared.

Think of any thing that is causing you anxiety or stress: Money shortage? Fear of being down sized? Can't lift as much weight at the gym as you used to? Try this exercise. Maybe you'll sleep better tonight.

Taking It Off

You most probably know that obesity is a serious health problem in North America. Here are some statistics:

- A study of 900,000 followed over 16 years showed that being overweight contributes to 20% of cancer deaths in women and 14% in men.
- 5% of high blood pressure in women and 78% in men can be attributed directly to obesity. High blood pressure leads to strokes and Alzheimer's.
- Colon cancer risk is up to 70% greater in overweight men.
- More than twenty million North Americans have obesity-related adult-onset diabetes, and more than one-third do not know it.
- Obese smokers die 13.5 years sooner than normal-weight non-smokers.
- Obese Americans spend 36% more on health-care than Americans of normal weight. (The figure is the same in Canada, but it is not as noticeable because Health Care picks up most of the tab.)

There are many weight loss programs around, but do some thorough researches before you try any. I mentioned before that Elizabeth and I have been eating in the 'Zone' for several years, and when I first started I lost 20 pounds in five months, and dropped my cholesterol level by 50%. I did this without feeling any hunger, and eating normal food. Over the years I got a bit lax, and gained about ten pounds back, but this program has given me the desire to be more aware of the amount I eat, and I know if I stay in the Zone, I will not get hungry. The basic concept of eating in the Zone is to balance your caloric intake of carbohydrates, fats and protein in the ratio of 40%-30%-30%. And to determine, through charts in the book, how much food you should eat, as measured by "exchanges" of food. Dr. Sears has published a number of books. The one we use is *The Zone*.

Now That You Lost It, How Do You Keep It Off?

It is one thing to lose weight, and quite another to keep it off. I believe there are two keys that will help keep me from gaining weight again:

- I exercise for an hour three times a week, doing a combination of cardio and weights.
- I will continue to eat "In the Zone"

Getting All Choked Up

I noticed around age fifty I became more emotional. I didn't know whether it was just me or if other men experienced the same thing.

A few years ago, I was a guest "expert" a number of times on a Canadian Broadcasting Corporation radio call-in show, talking about midlife men. When I mentioned having become more emotional, a lot of men said they were too, and it was good to know they weren't alone.

A friend said he gets choked up, even cries sometimes, when a news story shows people being rescued from some difficult situation, such as a fire or flood. Of course he tries to make sure nobody sees him.

In an article entitled *"Enormous Changes at the Last Moment: Men's Emotional Challenges at Midlife"*, (*http://www.mensresourcecenter.org/enormous_changes.html*) Kathleen W. Wilson, M.D., had this to say:

> As men move into their 40s and 50s, the connections among their brain cells actually increase in complexity. This translates into more thinking and feeling. The wonderful part of this is that it allows a man to change, no matter how emotionally limited his parents may have been, he can become more loving, positive, and generative as he ages.

> But sometimes these brain changes may affect a man's relationship with his wife or partner, in particular colliding with the irritability that affects many women at the same age. They may also engender feelings and thoughts that are uncomfortable: ruminations about the worth of one's life and occupation, questions about the direction one has taken and the choices one has made, confusion about what to do next, fears about growing older and facing death. These feelings can combine to create what we often call a "midlife crisis," with the potential for depression, affairs, and alcohol or drug addiction.

> Confusing and painful as they may be, these feelings, along with the "new freedom" of midlife, also have the

potential to transform men's lives into something healthier, more coherent and whole.

If you have been feeling more emotional, don't worry. It is
normal. Now that I am in my 60s, I find the emotional roller
coaster I went through during my 50s has settled down, but I
certainly experience a wider range of emotions than I did in my
40s and younger. I am less self-conscious about it than I used to
be, too. Maybe that is one reason grandchildren and grandfathers
have so much fun. They are unselfconscious enough be willing to
act silly, and let their feelings show.

Rippin' It Up – The Need for Fun

A few years ago, when I was in the depth of what Daniel Levinson, *The Seasons of a Man's Life* [3] calls, "the Age Fifty Transition,"
I did not have much fun. My wife Elizabeth, who was also going
through a major transition, and I, would often talk about how we
felt so serious all the time. It wasn't that we had lost our sense of
humour, but we just felt serious.

We enjoyed hiking, and as we lived in Vancouver, B.C. at the
time, we were near many great hikes in the mountains all around
Vancouver. We were part of a group that hiked on many weekends, and it was a source of renewal and recreation for us, and
even fun, as we hiked with a wonderful group of people. It helped
us get out of 'serious mode' from time to time.

I had another experience around that age, during my training
to become a personal/professional coach. One of the exercises
we did was a visit with our Future Self (ourselves, 20 years in the

---

[3] Levinson, Daniel; *The Seasons of a Man's Life*; Random House; New
York, NY; 1978.

future). It was a powerful experience for me, and at the end of the visit, my Future Self gave me an Otter. He explained it was a 'Cosmic Otter', and that it was to remind me to approach life from a sense of playfulness. That life is too important to take solemnly. It took a number of years before I felt playful again.

I have noticed the same tendency in most of the men I meet who are going through a challenging transition. Sometimes it just feels as though things are falling apart - your work is no longer satisfying, your marriage is feeling a little dull, and you feel irritable much of the time. Not exactly a fun experience. Yet fun and playfulness are very important, especially during challenging times.

Here is what William A. Sadler says about it in his excellent book, *The Third Age:*

> Play is important to growth at all ages. It is the source of our creativity. It is also important to health, not only as a form of therapy but as a form of healthy adult adaptation. Researcher Dr. Vaillant discovered that those best adapted to life in their fifties allowed more time for vacations than did the least-successfully adapted, who often found little or no vacation time.

> "Similarly, the reporter Peter Chew found that, "leisure was the key to men's eventual successful passage through the most critical years of their middle life."

> "Play is no less important to adults than to children. Human beings are not only Homo sapiens and Homo faber, but also Homo ludens - beings who are thinkers and workers and, pre-eminently, players. Play has fundamental importance to individual development; it is even a foundation of human culture. Play frees the human spirit

and provides the basis for the highest forms of human expression. If we are to become more open and creative as well as happier and more fulfilled we need to increase the element of play in our lives. We also need to infuse more of it into our work. That is a sure way to activate the child within us so that we can grow young.[4]

Going through a midlife transition can feel pretty heavy, and sometimes you need a break. So... get our there and rip it up. I am not talking about the most incredible fun you ever had, or hours of belly laughs, but just doing something light and playful – anything from literally playing with little kids (your grandchildren if you have any), to having a good conversation and a few laughs with your buddies.

Losing ZZZ's, Losing Cool

I don't know about you, but it has been a long time since I had the recommended eight hours of sleep. I know I am not alone. When I checked on the kinds of drugs people were buying when they clicked through to the online pharmacies I recommend on my *www.midlife-men.com* site, almost half the sales were for sleeping medications.

Dr. Matthew Walker is director of the Sleep and Neuroimaging Labortatory at the University of California, Berkeley. He and his colleagues did a study using 26 young adults, who were divided into two groups. One group stayed awake for 35 hours, and the other group got a normal night's sleep during the same period. Members of both groups then underwent brain scans

---

[4] Sandler, William; *The Third Age: 6 principles for Growth and Renewal After Forty*; Perseus Publishing; Cambridge, MA; 2000.

while they looked at 100 images that were increasingly negative, starting with neutral pictures of spoons or baskets, and moving to disturbing pictures of mutilated bodies and children with tumours.

Brain activity during this time was drastically different between the two groups. The difference was in the amygdala, which is the part of the brain responsible for emotional responses.

"In those who are sleep-deprived, the amygdala goes into a hyperdrive situation so that it is approximately 60 percent more reactive than in those who got a good night's sleep," said Dr. Walker, who published the research with colleagues from Harvard medical school.

Lack of sleep also inhibits the activity of the medial-prefrontal cortex of the brain, which normally put the brakes on the amygdala, he said. The bottom line: when you are tired, you are wired to be cranky.

When I was in my early fifties, I noticed I was more irritable than I used to be. Things that never used to upset me, or at least upset me very little, would suddenly cause a flash of anger. As guest on a CBC talk show, I mentioned my newfound irritability and the phone board lit up with callers saying they were experiencing the same thing. They were relieved to know they weren't alone! Wives called in wondering what they could do about their husbands, who used to be nice, and were now, as one woman described, "like living with an angry brick."

An article by Celia Milne in the national Canadian paper *The Globe and Mail* talked about how a lack of sleep can make us grouchy. All kinds of bad things can happen when you are tired. Snapping at your wife or kids is never very productive, but road rage, mistakes and accidents on the job, and high staff turnover

(due to grouchy bosses), are some other costly consequences of
sleep loss.

We are busier now than we have ever been, and according to
Statistics Canada, almost half the population admits to voluntari-
ly cutting down on sleep. Not to mention the one in seven who is
an insomniac.

If you're finding yourself over-irritable without an easy explanation, this might be a symptom of sleep deprivation. Pay
attention and get some more sleep.

> Jed Diamond, in his book, *The Irritable Male Syndrome: Understand-*
> *ing and Managing the 4 Key Causes of Depression and Aggression,*
> describes a number of other reasons for irritability at midlife. See
> "Section One: Fine-Tuning The Mind, Cutting Down on Skid Marks."

Sex, Money and Happiness

In spite of the old adage that "Money can't bring you happiness",
everybody I know is pretty sure having more money would make
THEM happier.

So what do you do when you don't have more money, and
don't see your ship coming in any time soon? Well, a couple of
economists in the U.S. have determined that in the happiness
department, sex can be just as good as money. In fact, they have
been able to make some direct comparisons, which I will tell you
about in a minute.

David G. Blanchflower and Andrew J. Oswald surveyed a random sample of 16,000 adult Americans to study the links between income, sexual behaviour and reported happiness. They
reported their findings in a paper called *"Money, Sex and Happi-*

ness: An Empirical Study", published by the National Bureau of
Economic Research in Cambridge, Maryland, last May.

Here are some of their findings:

- Frequency of sexual activity is shown to be positively associated with happiness. This is true for males and females, and for those under and over the age of 40.

- The median American has sexual intercourse 2-3 times a month (among people under 40 years of age, the median amount of sex is once a week). Approximately 6% of the population report having sex more than three times a week.

- Almost half of American women over the age of 40 report they did not have sexual intercourse in the previous year. The figure for men is 20%.

- Homosexual and bisexual people make up about 2.5% of the United States population, and homosexuality has no statistically significant effects on happiness.

- Sex seems to have disproportionately strong effects on the happiness of highly educated people.

- The happiest people were those that had only one regular sexual partner the previous year.

- Married people have more sex than those who are single, divorced, widowed, or separated.

- Highly educated females tend to have fewer sexual partners.

- Income has no effect. Money buys neither more sexual partners nor more sex.

Now here's the interesting part...

Using a combination of formulae only economists could come
up with, they found that sex "enters so strongly (and) positively

in happiness equations" that they estimate increasing intercourse from once a month to once a week is equivalent to the amount of happiness generated by making an extra $50,000 a year for the average American.

They also determined that a good, stable marriage brings as much happiness as making an extra $100,000 per year.

Divorce, on the other hand, reduced happiness by the equivalent of losing $66,000 a year.

Now, does sex lead to happiness, or are happy people just more likely to lead each other to the bedroom? That's still under investigation, say the economists, but there is evidence that psyche and sex feed off each other.

A down-turning economy forces many to worry about the loss of money through lay-offs, cutbacks and investments. It's a good idea to focus on the thing that can make you happiest: money or sex, you pick? You know what to do (if you can get your wife/partner to go along with it).

Live Like the Wind's in Your Hair

Don't Stop Rockin'

Research shows that a fit 70-year-old who has remained active can be as strong as an unfit sedentary 30-year-old. In fact, an active person will decline physiologically only by about half a per cent a year compared to an inactive person who will decline by about 2 per cent. If there is one thing that will serve us well as we age, it is physical fitness.

According to Michael F. Roizen, MD; Professor of Anaesthesiology and Internal Medicine, SUNY Upstate Medical Center in

New York, there is well-quantified research to show that physical fitness benefits you in three major areas:

- It reduces arterial aging, which is associated with memory loss, impotence, heart disease, stroke, reduced orgasm quality, even wrinkling of the skin.
- It slows down immune aging, which is associated with infections and cancer, and autoimmune disease such as many forms of arthritis.
- It reduces accidents and disability from accidents.

And here are a few more benefits you gain from regular exercise:

- Increased Strength
- Increased Bone Density (this matters more as we age)
- Increased Ability to Handle Stress (a biggy during midlife transitions!)
- Increased Flexibility (again, increasingly important as we get older)

SO... that being said, how does one establish a *regular* exercise routine? (Maybe you too have an exercise bike or treadmill acting as a clothes hanger in the basement?) You know how it is. Something - maybe a New Year's resolution or maybe your favourite pants just got a bit too tight - triggers you to start an exercise routine. Or maybe you just want to be more trim so you will be considered for that promotion to senior manager (research shows that anything above a 34 inch waist reduces your chances of promotion). You get all revved up and buy an exercise machine, or maybe join a fitness club. You go at it hammer and tong for a session or two, your muscles get sore, and pretty soon you have missed a workout, then another, and then it's gone.

WELL, here's what the experts say: *If you have not been working out, DON'T START WITH STAMINA EXERCISES.* Start with something easier, like a 30-minute walk or 20 minutes of stretching. Maybe you can throw in a few isometrics while you watch you favourite TV show. Once you build up a bit of conditioning, you might think of increasing the intensity. Maybe that's when you join the fitness club.

What works for me is a circuit training class. I work out three times a week. Knowing I will be working with others in an organized routine that works out all my muscle groups and revs up my heart and lungs for a while, is enough to motivate me to go. I am self-employed, so my schedule is flexible enough to allow me to get to the gym during the day. I don't always enjoy the workout, and sometimes I have to force myself to go, but I always enjoy the benefits.

Here's the other key: Build exercise into your regular routine, and see it as part of your normal life from now on, not something you do "if you have time." And remember... it takes a while for the benefits to show up, but show up they will.

Zoomers

Zoomers are really Boomers (anyone born after 1946) with their foot on the accelerator – they're souped-up! Zoomers have the body of a 65-year-old, the mind of a 45-year-old, the libido of a 35-year-old, and the heart of a teenager. Apparently Zoomers control 1/2 all North American wealth!

I think they got the data a little bit incorrect in that the body should be of about a 52-year-old if it is an average-aged boomer, as the boomer generation is from about 1946-1966. I like the idea of being a Zoomer (even though I am not officially a Boomer, having been born in 1945). At any rate, the idea is that the boomer generation is different than any before it.

Zoomers are:

- better educated
- healthier
- faced little hardship, and many opportunities while growing up
- worships youthfulness, and refuses to admit to aging

If you are a Zoomer, you have the energy, education, confidence and health to continue being actively engaged in the world for a long time yet. The difference as you age is that your emotional focus changes. You are more interested in societal change and spiritual growth. It is similar to the idealism of your teenage years, but with the experience and wisdom that comes with age.

Experts say that fifty is the new forty, and sixty is the new fifty. Zoomers have changed the world during every stage of their lives, and don't appear to be stopping now.

The only cautionary note comes from Yang Yang, an assistant professor in the Department of Sociology at the University of Chicago, in a 2008 study on aging and happiness reported in the *American Sociological Review* (73:204-226, 2008). Yang found that as we get older, we are in general happier, and the oldest among us are the happiest. Except for Zoomers that is, who are the least happy! Linda George, an aging expert at Duke University, speculates that the reason for this is that Boomers/Zoomers are not lowering their aspirations as they age, the way earlier generations have. They still think they should have it all, and they think retirement will let them do everything they haven't done yet. The reality is that isn't going to happen, and it makes Zoomers less satisfied than they could be.

So, relax into your older age. There are things you wanted to do when you were younger, and you are simply not going to do them. Accept it. Then find something you are still passionate about, and that you CAN do, and hop to it.

Back-Up Your Face

A few years ago I read an article about a prestigious plastic surgery clinic in Montreal, Quebec, where the famous and/or wealthy went to get face-lifts and so forth. What surprised me (perhaps I am naive) was that the majority of this clinic's clients were men, usually senior executives, in their fifties and older. These men knew that if they started looking old, they would lose power, and be torn apart by the young tigers climbing the ladder behind them who wanted their positions.

I don't think the average man is going to get a face-lift (am I being naive again?), but I do think we do what we can to look as young as possible, and I think that is a pity.

In his book, *What Are Old People For? How Elders Will Save The World,* William H. Thomas, M.D. talks about our society's desperation to appear young, and the billions we spend on cosmetics, surgery and Botox injections. He includes an interesting quote from Marilyn Monroe from the book, *The Force of Character,* by James Hillman.

Monroe said, "I want to grow old without facelifts. They take the life out of a face, the character. I want to have the courage to be loyal to the face I've made." Considering the industry she lived in that would have taken courage, indeed.

Are you being loyal to the face you've made?

No doubt you have noticed, as I have, that as we age, our character and life experiences are increasingly reflected in our faces. By the time we get to our late forties and beyond, our faces begin to show the lines and creases brought about by the struggles we faced, the sorrows we suffered, the attitudes we hold toward life, and even the devious things we do.

These are not apparent in our youth, but as psychologist James Hillman says "...after sixty especially... A face is being made, often against your will, as witness to your character."

When you look in the mirror, do you like the face you see being made there? Is it an honest, open, happy face? A wise face? A compassionate face? Or perhaps a stressed, worried, harried, or even unkind face?

Here is the good news: if you don't like the face you are making, you can change it, but it is an inside job. It requires looking inside yourself for your truth, for the meaning of your life, figuring out what is important, maybe even clarifying your life mission, and then living the values you find there.

This is difficult work, and in my opinion, one of the major tasks we face at midlife. Often we need help in the form of personal growth workshops, spiritual retreats, or psychotherapy. You might also explore the "Your Life Mission" section of my website for some exercises (http://www.midlife-men.com/lifemission.html).

You may have met older men whose bitter, resentful, or victimized attitudes shows in their faces. Take a moment, step in front of a mirror. What kind of face are you making?

A great organization for helping us become more truly men, and discover our sense of mission, is The ManKind Project's *New Warrior Training Adventure* weekends throughout North America, and in the UK, France, Germany, South Africa and Australia. http://mankindproject.org/

Having a Longer Happier Life

Look on the Bright Side - You'll Live Longer

This article is adapted from *Bottom Line's Daily Health News*: [5]

Learning to look at the glass as half full instead of half empty may add years to your life, and happier ones at that. In a study that followed adults for forty years - from their college days to the present - researchers found that optimists were far less likely to die young than their more pessimistic peers.

About the study

In the mid-1960s, more than 7,000 students at the University of North Carolina at Chapel Hill took a personality test that included questions that measured whether they were optimistic or pessimistic. While most of the participants fell somewhere in the middle, 1,630 were considered to be pessimists and 923 to be optimists. Tracking them over the next four decades, researchers discovered that the most pessimistic study participants had a 42% greater likelihood of dying from any cause than the most optimistic participants. These results were published in

---

[5] Adapted with the permission of: Bottom Line Publications, Boardroom Inc. 281 Tresser Blvd., 8th Floor Stamford, CT 06901 *www.BottomLineSecrets.com*

the December 2006 issue of the *Mayo Clinic Proceedings* medical journal.

Look on the bright side

Charles S. Carver, PhD, a psychology professor at the University of Miami, has found that optimism plays an important role in how successfully people cope with stressful experiences. Dr. Carver speculates that the reasons behind this startling difference in life expectancy likely include:

a. Optimists tend to take better care of themselves than pessimists (e.g., paying greater attention to maximizing health through lifestyle considerations such as diet and exercise).

b. Pessimists often worry too much, and numerous research studies have shown that stress and anxiety are themselves health risks for many conditions, especially cardiovascular disease.

Dr. Carver says pessimists can learn to put a more positive spin on their lives. He says cognitive therapy, which focuses specifically on changing outlook, is effective for many people. Practices such as meditation, yoga or Pilates, and keeping a "gratitude journal" can be useful as well.

I agree. I have exercised regularly - I exercise and do Pilates, and have prayed and meditated for many years. My cup always looks half full (or even fuller) to me. If yours looks half empty, maybe some therapy, and some of the practices mentioned here can help. You'll live longer, and have more fun while you are alive.

Grow Young, Not Old

The famous psychologist, Carl Jung believed that "in every adult there lurks a child - an eternal child, something that is always becoming, is never completed, and calls for unceasing care, attention, and education." Jung believed that the process of individuation - becoming your own person - constitutes "the only meaningful life." In his view, reactivating one's inner child is the ultimate measure of success; it represents nothing less than a vocation.

Jung himself had a serious midlife crisis. He was a protégé of Sigmund Freud, and Freud saw him as the disciple who would carry on his work. But when Jung was in his forties, he suddenly realized he didn't want to be Freud's disciple. He had his own ideas about psychology, and he needed to follow his own path. He broke with Freud, which was painful for both of them, and set out on a journey of discovery.

I have heard a similar pattern in many men I have talked to. Many ended up changing jobs in midlife, and those who stayed found ways to do their work so it was more fulfilling and less stressful. You can find some of these men's stories on the 'Men's Stories' page on my website: *www.midlife-men.com/mens-stories.html*

Here is a typical story of such a man as described by William A. Sadler:

Matthew: "I had this strange dream. . . a child looked at me with reproach. I realized I had to take care of the child within me."

Matthew helped me see more clearly the paradox of growing young while simultaneously accepting age and one's own mortality. A fifty-four year-old Canadian educator when I first interviewed him, Matthew told me that he was in the best period of his life: happily married with three talented children; in charge of a distinctive university program supported by grants; recognized for his leadership in his community; in good health and physically active in several sports. To my surprise I learned that if I had interviewed him several years earlier, I would have found him in dire straits:

Matthew: I think I've changed a lot in the past few years. About eight years ago I felt trapped. I could see that everything was going well. My marriage was good, the family was developing, my job was right, and I was in good health. But I started to feel like the floor had been taken away from underneath me.

I was confronting the meaning of my life. What am I doing? What is the purpose of my life? For some reason I felt empty inside. I thought, "If I were to die tomorrow I wouldn't care." What had been so important, my career and my competence just didn't seem to be enough.

I went to a therapist for about a year. Through this process I discovered that I had been giving too much importance to professional activity and external achievements. I had been ignoring some very important aspects of myself.

In particular, I had neglected my childhood qualities: playfulness, imagination, and creativity. At that time I had this strange dream that kept recurring. I saw a child who looked at me with reproach, as though it was my fault that he was dying. Sometimes the child would be lying in a coffin. I would reach out to embrace him, and then he would revive. Finally, I sensed that I was that child. I realized I had to take care of the child within me. I still have much to learn about this and to allow more time for play, imagination, and reflection.[6]

At midlife, regret, hormonal changes, dissatisfaction with our work or life can turn us into grumpy old couch potatoes. Now is the time to explore new options. Get some exercise. It keeps the circulation healthy, which in turn feeds the brain and the spirit. Then ask yourself how you are doing in the playfulness department. Are you taking things more seriously than necessary? Lift your spirits by paying a little more attention to the child within you. Learn to play again. Take up art, writing, learning to play a musical instrument or any number of other hobbies in order to stimulate your imagination and creativity. Spend more time with your kids and especially with your grandchildren. Seeing the world through their eyes gives you back your youth. Playing with them keeps you active.

Simply relax and do something you like. The idea is to "die young - as late as possible".

---

[6] William A. Sadler; The Third Age: Six Principles for Personal Growth and Rejuvenation after Forty; Perseus Publishing; Cambridge, MA; 2000. exerpt pp 88-89:

SECTION THREE

Fuel Your Spiritual Potential

Filling the Vacuum

Down through the ages people have tried to figure out how to have meaningful and fulfilling lives. For centuries, it was thought that following the rules of the government and the church was the way. Now many people are disillusioned with both, and are feeling lost.

This leads to a certain amount of confusion. You may not be used to using your internal guidance system as a standard, and you resist the personal responsibility it calls for. Many people are left with a kind of "personal vacuum" which they try to fill with all kinds of things: material goods, sex, booze, food, busyness – anything to make the empty feeling go away. At midlife, men are especially prone to this. (Over the years, I have tried most of the above!)

But the feeling won't go away until the right action is taken: seeking spiritual growth and development.

Science has hindered spiritual development, saying either the spiritual realm doesn't exist, or doesn't matter. Many people have bought that story, and tried to find meaning in other ways.

Religion has hindered spiritual growth as well, by failing to update itself. Its principles are sound, but all its stories are old, out-of-date, and difficult for people in our society to relate to. It is as though religions are saying that all the important stuff happened a long time ago, and we need to keep going back for guidance and stories to learn by, when there are new stories to learn from every day. So you face a dilemma, how to go forward when your main guidance systems – religion and science – aren't able to guide us.

The best way to begin is with intention. Become clear about what you are looking for. Intend to have a relationship with The Creator, and then seek knowledge and take action. As you move forward with clear intention in your heart, you will find the guidance you need as you go along.

It may mean finding a spiritual guide, or studying the advice of spiritual leaders from the past. You don't need to limit yourself to one guide. For some prayer and meditation are good, for others community service, and for yet others contemplation or fasting. (I do a four-day waterless fast every year that is the spiritual highlight of my year.)

I had a "spiritual awakening" in 1983 that dramatically changed my life for the better. Since then, I have continued to study and grow spiritually, and my life has continued to improve.

No matter what approach you use, when you set out with clear intention your life becomes more peaceful, filled with love, and balanced.

Shot by a Sacred Bullet

Sometimes things happen that cause you to look at what you are doing with your life. You could think of these things as "Sacred Bullets" that impale or puncture you so you will have a "Sacred Wound" on which to focus your attention. It wakes you from the distractions of daily life.

The Sacred Bullet may come in the form of a sickness, job loss, separation or divorce, or some other trauma such as an accident. Sacred Bullets are not harmful, but they do poke holes in your illusions.

Once a Sacred Bullet hits you, it is necessary to examine the wound and search inside for what caused it. What are you missing, or not paying attention to, in your life? What busy-ness is distracting you from your Soul's purpose, or keeping you from waking up?

Sacred Bullets are gifts, but they can appear to be life-threatening.

You struggle through your days, pursuing earthly tasks such as making a living (which must be done) while putting off the tasks of learning the true meaning of living in the world.

Whenever you act from your heart - helping a stranger in need, contributing to a good cause, lifting up a downcast person with words of encouragement, spreading love in the world through acts of kindness and compassion - you are teaching yourself the secrets of life, even if you are unaware it is happening in your subconscious.

If you consciously attempt to learn these secrets through "right living" as well as prayer, meditation and surrender to God as you understand Him, your learning is faster. Paradoxically, as you grow spiritually you get shot with bigger Sacred Bullets, as you are able to handle bigger wounds. These bury themselves even deeper to help you see the most subtle illusions about your life.

When you experience pain, frustration, sorrow or other trials in your life, look inside for the message. Maybe it is a Sacred Bullet directing your attention at something.

Love Nudges from Your Inner Voice

I believe one of the main tasks of midlife and beyond is spiritual growth. You may connect more consciously with the Higher Power through church, meditation, prayer, communing with nature, or any of a variety of other approaches.

One of the tangible benefits of going on the spiritual journey is to receive messages from what I call your "inner voice." In the Bible there is reference to the "still, small voice of God." I suspect this is the same voice I am talking about.

I find this voice very useful for getting guidance in puzzling circumstances, and for keeping my life on track in general. As I have mentioned before, every year since 1990 I go through a four-day waterless fast. This is the spiritual highlight of my year, and the time I am most likely to receive a message from my Inner Voice. It usually arrives in my thoughts as a brief sentence or two, with some clarity for staying on the spiritual path in the coming year. It has a different tone than my normal self-talk, and I have never found it to be wrong. I often get a brief message from it during times of stress, or confusion.

Here is an example: When my wife and I were moving to Vancouver in 1997, we flew there one Saturday morning to look for a place to rent. We had decided we could pay a maximum of $1600 per month, plus utilities. Elizabeth had drawn up a list of things she wanted in a house, which looked fine to me. We looked at houses all day, and at the end of the day, we found one we wanted to rent. We filled out the application, and were told by the current tenants that the landlord would likely go to church the next morning then call us for an interview. He said he was sure we had a good chance of being able to rent the house.

The next morning we ate breakfast, then went back to the room expecting a call. None came. We were confident we would get the house, but thought we had better keep looking just in case. Off and on during the day we called the hotel for messages, but there were none. Still we expected to get the house.

As the day wore on, I began to feel depressed, and I didn't know why, although I knew it had something to do with the house. When we got back to the hotel, the message light was blinking so I called the desk, and she explained that we had received a call that morning, but for some reason, our room's answering machine had malfunctioned for that one call. It turned out the landlord had called to interview us, and when we didn't return his call, he rented it to the only other couple he was interviewing.

I immediately began to feel better! The whole situation was puzzling to me, so I did a brief meditation and asked for some clarity. Within a few minutes, I got this message from the Inner Voice: *"Your house is not ready yet, and the middle of the month is an important date".* I wasn't sure what that meant, but I trusted it was true.

The upshot was that when I was back in Vancouver a couple of weeks later, I found the upper two stories of a duplex across the street from the ocean, with wonderful views of the bay and the mountains beyond. The first house didn't have a view and that had caused my depression. Here I was being given more light and beauty and it rented for $1680, including utilities. Exactly the amount of money we had decided we could afford. It had come on the rental market on the 15th, which was why on the 1st, "our house wasn't ready yet, and the middle of the month was an important date!"

How to tap in to your Inner Voice

We can access the knowledge and wisdom of what I will call our Higher Self, (although I don't know what exactly the source of this knowledge is), through silence, quieting our mind, and allowing the information to come through. It can be useful to ask a short, concise question.

The answer may come as a short sentence, or an insight suddenly appearing in our mind, as a body sensation (a rush of energy when we have a certain thought as we ask about the situation), or even a message from another person, as we hold ourselves open to the answer we are seeking. You have no doubt had someone remind you of something you said years before that changed his or her life, and you have no recollection of even having said it. Or perhaps you received a message that way. It is as though you are used by a high power to deliver messages from time to time.

However you do it, my experience tells me the most important steps are:

- Accept that receiving guidance from some higher source is possible.
- Prepare yourself by having a clear question in mind, or simply by opening yourself to receive guidance.
- Find a quiet place to still your mind, and wait. I find breath counting can be useful in quieting my mind. Breath counting is simply done by counting each breath as it comes in and goes out. I try to do ten breaths with no thought entering my mind. If a thought comes along, I simply let it go, and start the counting again from 'one'. I find that once I get to 'ten' without a thought, my mind is quiet.
- Do not have an agenda for what the answer should be. Be open to whatever comes to you.
- When you receive the answer, ponder it to see whether it seems reasonable (sometimes our minds will play games with us), and perhaps talk it over with someone whose wisdom and integrity you trust.

Your Inner Voice is a valuable tool in guiding you through the difficult situations in your life. Pick it up and use it.

Stand Down For a Day

Remember when stores used to be closed on Sundays and Mondays or Sundays and Wednesdays, as they were in my hometown? Even in cities, stores and businesses used to be closed on Sundays, and people generally relaxed that day. A year ago I drove through an American city where the stores were closed on Sunday. I was shocked! I haven't seen that in a Canadian city for a long time.

The Bible says God instructed us to have a day of rest, and set an example, as well. Most of us don't stop for "The Sabbath" any more. Even if we don't work on Sundays, we are usually busy trying to catch up with family chores before we go back to work on Monday. But maybe all that busy-ness is killing us.

A research study done in Israel back in the late 1980s compared a bunch of Orthodox (read practicing) Jews with a similar group of Jews who did not observe the Sabbath. All other conditions were pretty much the same (i.e. lifestyle, type of work, socio-economic class, etc.). The study found that the group that strictly observed the Sabbath had a lower rate of heart disease.

The physiological reason for this is that during your normal active life you produce and/or ingest lipids (various kinds of fatty acids, triglycerides and steroids that are essential for health, but need to be 'managed' by your bodies). Lipids build up in the blood faster than your liver can burn them off. A day of rest gives your liver a chance to catch up. Without it, you suffer.

If you do take it easy at least one day a week, you'll improve your chances for fighting off disease and you'll feel better.

Jettison Your Junk

When I was a kid growing up in rural Alberta, very few people had indoor plumbing on their farms, and even fewer had electricity. Every now and then the government would do a survey and announce that a lot of people were still living below the poverty line, as they did not have indoor plumbing or electricity. We thought it was a joke. Maybe we had to use the little brown shack out back, but we certainly never thought of ourselves as being poverty-stricken. In fact we felt sorry for the town kids that didn't have a farm to live on.

In the western world, we are so hooked on 'stuff', that we frequently sacrifice quality of life in order to get more stuff. Standard of living is essentially a measure of material wealth.

We often confuse it with quality of life.

The good news is that by the time you reach your middle years, you are starting to figure out this conundrum, and are beginning to pay some attention to the other things that create fulfilment.

After you have enough stuff, you can increase your quality of life indefinitely by such things as having good relationships with the people in your lives, learning new skills (hobbies, etc.), becoming masterful at what you do, having a sense of personal mission, spiritual growth, and belonging to a club or service organization.

Pursuing the things that are satisfying for you makes your life more fulfilling. It shouldn't cost a lot of money, because the intangibles like joy, fulfillment and love are free.

The Truths of Life

A good story has a different meaning for each reader or listener, so the interpretation of a story by an expert, although interesting, is no more valid than your own interpretation. I love myths and folktales because they tell, in metaphoric or symbolic form, the truths of life. I have read hundreds of folktales, and have discovered there are certain patterns that are repeated in tales from different ages and cultures. Carl Jung would call them archetypal patterns.

One pattern features a hero, usually a young man, who ends up in a big house or castle that is owned by a man, or sometimes an old woman, with some daughters – usually up to three. To me, this pattern tells the story of the 'non-intuitive' nature of spiritual growth.

The hero in these stories is given three impossible tasks by the owner of the mansion who, although hospitable, turns out to be a wizard, or some other powerful but evil character. The hero is then approached secretly by the daughter, or if there are more than one, the youngest daughter, who gives him secret information about how to accomplish the impossible task.

For example, the task might be to clear a thicket of shrubs or trees. The wizard will offer the hero two axes - one which is new and sharp, the other which is dull and rusty and full of nicks. The daughter will instruct the hero to choose the dull axe. But the hero, being ego-driven, will choose the new axe.

When he goes to clear the thicket, the trees grow back faster than he can cut them. At midday the daughter comes to see how he is doing, and tells him he should have chosen the dull axe as she suggested. She then tells him to lie down and rest, and she finishes the job for him.

The same thing happens with each of the tasks he is given... the hero chooses the wrong tool (the one that makes sense from a logical point of view) and the daughter has to finish the task for him. It may be emptying a well with a leaky pail, or cleaning out a cow shed with a broken down shovel, or some other seemingly impossible task.

After the youth, who has accomplished the tasks with the help of the daughter (in some cases it is just a young woman who has been captured by the wizard and his wife), has finished all the tasks (normally three), he is given permission to marry the daughter the next day.

The daughter tells him they must flee that night because the wizard plans to kill them. She instructs the young hero to go to the barn and saddle the skinniest horse, but again the youth chooses the best-looking horse, leaving the skinniest, which is the fastest, for the wizard to ride when trying to catch up to them. They flee, and when, sometime later in the night, the wizard discovers they are gone and comes after them, the daughter uses her magical powers to create obstacles for the Maybe she tells the youth to reach onto the horse's ear, where he finds various items, which he throws behind them. He might find a comb, which when he throws behind them becomes an impenetrable forest, forcing the wizard to go back for his magic axe. As they flee they throw other things, usually three in all, which create obstacles such as mountain ranges and rivers as well as forests.

The young couple eventually outruns the wizard, or he drowns in the lake they create, and they get back to the young man's home village. He leaves her at the edge of town, goes to greet his family, and then forgets about her.

Some time passes, and he is about to marry a girl from town when the young woman comes along and helps him remember her, and they get married.

In this kind of story the young woman represents your inner or spiritual nature, which can help you accomplish what your ego self can never do. It has magical power, but the ego, represented by the boy's choices and by the evil wizard, is threatened by this magical power which demands surrender to 'higher knowledge,' fearing its own death.

It seems counter-intuitive to choose the broken-down tools, but the spiritual path demands surrender, not logic.

Spiritual experiences can seem subtle even though they are real. You may even tend to discount, or forget them, just as the young man forgets the girl that saved his life when he gets back to the real world of his village and family.

But spiritual experiences must be recognized and honoured if they are to have a useful role in your life, and in the folktales, the youth eventually does remember the young woman and marries her or takes her into his life.

Soul Task Number One:
The Breakdown of the Persona

In 1982 a group from the L'Arche Community (http://www.larche.ca/) in Edmonton went to Japan as part of an exchange with an organization there. I was asked to go along as a journalist and report on the trip. As I did my cultural research before going, I was struck by the emphasis Japanese people put on what class of work they do - labour, blue collar, white collar, and so forth.

One of the first young men I met when I got there, when asked what he did, said, with great pride, that he was a white collar worker. It struck me that Japanese people live somewhat restricted lives in that they are stuck with the label of what they do. I didn't realize at the time that we get just as stuck.

Here in the Western world, we spend the first half of our life building a "persona" in a sense, becoming who we are. As men usually focus on occupation, you might say "I am a carpenter" or "I am an accountant," or an "IT specialist," or whatever.

You take pride in your ability. You are "a skilful carpenter," or "an honest accountant," or "an IT specialist that can solve any technical problem."

At the same time, you may become a husband, father, uncle, friend, maybe business partner. All of these things together, along with others such as the social, sports or hobby groups you join, your role in community life, and perhaps your affiliations with religious organizations, make up your Persona.

Over time, as you become better at your trade, and more active and better known in the organizations to which you belong, and in your community, you not only gain status and position, but slowly, almost imperceptibly, you begin to feel restricted and boxed in. The idea of changing occupations or social groups begins to sound frightening. You may change jobs, but not occupations. The more socially significant your position (lawyer, doctor, priest), the more your role will restrict your growth. It is not that this box is bad. In fact it is essential. But at midlife it may become the wrong box, and if we try to stay in it when it no longer fits, it can become a prison.

Who would you be if you were no longer "the plumber people can depend on," or "the honest mechanic who knows everything about cars," "the trusted minister" or "the teacher who inspires kids to learn?"

If you try to change, your friends, family, co-workers, and even community at large (especially if you are in a socially prominent job) will try to stop you. They will try reason ("Why would you start over now, Bob? You have so much to lose."), threats ("If you leave this job, you will never get one with another company"), pleading ("You are such a great minister. We need you. You can't leave us."), and even anger ("You are the most self-centred person I know. Think about us. We depend on you.").

In a way, your prison has become so familiar and safe to you, you are reluctant to leave, as this section of *The Prisoner of Chillon* by Lord Byron describes so well:

It was at length the same to me,
Fetter'd or fetterless to be,
I learn'd to love despair.
And thus when they appear'd at last,
And all my bonds aside were cast,
These heavy walls to me had grown
A hermitage-and all my own!
And half I felt as they were come
To tear me from a second home:
... My very chains and I grew friends,
So much a long communion tends
To make us what we are: even I
Regain'd my freedom with a sigh.

But if you are to continue your growth as a human being, and become "fully alive," you must look with clear-eyed honesty at the persona you have created, and be willing let it go, so you can create a new, more authentic version of yourself for the next stage of your life. It can be a challenging and unhappy time.

Accept That You Are the Only One Steering Your Ship

At this point in life, it is easy, and indeed common, for a man to blame others for his predicament. He would be much happier if only: his wife wasn't nagging him all the time, or was more interested in him; his family didn't take him for granted and see him just as the faceless drudge that brings home the money; his boss wasn't such a jerk, and appreciated his efforts more; I could go on, but you get the idea.

This is a dangerous time for you, because if you get caught in blaming others for your unhappiness, you are likely to quit your job, quit your marriage, or both, get a new job, get into a new relationship, or both. You might become the middle aged man acquiring a hot sports car, and a hotter young girlfriend; a stereotype of a man trying to stay in his persona. But when the newness of the new circumstances wears off, you are no happier than before.

The only way through is in. You do not have to change your job, or spouse, or anything else. But you do have to change your focus – from persona-oriented (looking for meaning and validation outside yourself), to self-oriented (looking inward for meaning and validation).

Nothing else will do.

Soul Task Number Two:
Finding Our Shadows

As you are taught how to 'be' in the world, you begin to hide parts of yourself away. They become your shadows. You learn useful things from your parents like, "It is not acceptable to kill your brother," but also things that are not useful such as, "Quit being such a smart aleck." Your exuberance and self-confidence hides from hurtful words: "Can't you do anything right?" "Here, let me do that for you."

You are not aware of creating your shadows, and when they are created you cannot see them in yourself. You see them reflected in others, but do not recognize them as your own. Dealing with shadows is tricky.

Babies have no shadows. They also have no self-restraint. They have to learn it. The world would be a scary place if we grew up to be as unrestrained as babies! We need to be socialized, in order to live successfully with others.

Your teachers get in on the act: "Don't sing, just mouth the words." Your creativity and love of music takes a hit, and your honest expression of anger goes into the "shadow bag" you drag around with you. "Good children don't get angry so easily." You get thousands of messages, and by the time you finish grade school, you have cut off big chunks of your natural self, and stuffed them in the shadow bag - the good with the bad.

At midlife, you need to make friends with your shadows. It is hard work.

Your Dark Shadows

One of the things I like about the *ManKind Project*, which sponsors, among other things, The New Warrior Training Adventure, is that the men in this organization recognize the need to deal with their shadows. It is never fun to search for and find one of your Dark Shadows, but you always benefit from doing so.

The easiest way to discover your shadows, both dark and golden, is to pay attention to other people who irritate you, or whom you judge negatively or very positively. You project the disowned parts of yourself onto those around you, as others do to you. We are simply mirrors for each other.

For years, I responded to arrogant people. I found them disgusting, and wanted to put them down at every opportunity. When I was in a group that included a person whom I considered arrogant, I would mention to a friend in the same group what an arrogant jerk that person was. I would often be amazed when my friend didn't think the other person was arrogant at all. Of course it turned out I was projecting my disowned arrogance onto the 'arrogant' person in the group.

Are there certain types of people who 'jerk your chain?' People you judge to be bullies, wimps, devious, dishonest, mean, cruel, thoughtless, tiresome, or any of dozens of other negative traits? Pay attention. Notice these judgements of yours. They are your ticket to a fuller, more authentic self.

When you find yourself reacting negatively to something someone has done, and whom you judge negatively (say a man at work seems to be always discounting your efforts, and you judge him to be uncaring), ask yourself, "What kind of man would act in that way?" Would it be: a cruel man, a thoughtless man, a man afraid to give praise to others in case it takes attention away from him, or a man who is himself never praised, and therefore holds his praise back from others?

Whatever you come up with, look back in your own life to the first time your efforts went unrecognized. Who was involved? Chances are it was a parent, or a teacher, or some other important adult from your childhood.

What did you hide away when that happened? Your righteous anger? Your hurt? Perhaps it was your exuberant young self who decided great effort wasn't worth it, or maybe you decided you had to work really hard all the time to try to earn recognition.

Then, ask yourself if you have ever withheld praise and recognition from others. Be honest with yourself. If you have, own that piece of yourself. Describe this shadow to at least one other person. It will help make you free. You will also notice that the people who 'hooked you' no longer do.

Golden Shadows

You don't just have Dark Shadows. Disown the dark parts of yourself. Are there people you greatly admire? People you would like to emulate? These are people you are projecting your 'golden shadows' onto.

Here is an example: if in grade one a teacher tells you that colouring outside the lines is wrong, you may begin to hide your creativity away. You then project your creative urges onto others, whom you think of as 'real' artists whose work you admire. This is one of your Golden Shadows. Midlife is a good time to rediscover your Golden Shadows, such as your own creativity.

Your Shadows, both Golden and Dark, are your wounds. You will likely never uncover all of them, but the more you expose, the better your relationships with yourself and others will be, and the more fully human and fully alive you will become. It is part of the path to elderhood. Those who continue to deny their shadows, and expect others (especially their wives, bosses, and other important people in their lives) to make them happy, will become elderly, but never Elders.

As you discover, and reclaim, the disowned shadow parts of yourself, you can continue on to the next task at midlife – "The Encounter with the Soul Mate."

Soul Task Number Three: Encountering Your Soul Mate

Psychologist Carl Jung's definition of the soul mate was what he called the "Anima" (feminine form), and "Animus" (masculine form), which comes from the Latin, meaning soul. They are somewhat ambiguous terms, hard to precisely define, but can be experienced.

It seems each man has his own "ideal feminine" template in his psyche. No one knows where this comes from, but it shows itself when you meet a woman who suddenly "lights your world."

It is as though your subconscious mind compares women to its ideal template, and when you see a woman that is a good match, it shouts, "There she is!"

In *Crossing the Soul's River*, William O. Roberts, Jr.[7] talks about four forms of the feminine:

* *Eve* - the mother of all
* *Helen* - the face that launched a thousand ships
* *Mary* - the spiritual companion
* *Sophia* - wisdom herself [7]

In your lifetime you have two great transitions: adolescence, and middle age.

Until adolescence, the ideal woman is your mother. At adolescence, you begin to discover *Helen*, the beautiful and desirable lover. During your twenties, you normally marry, embark on a career, and start a family. The woman you marry is usually a combination of both *Eve* and *Helen*.

During the busy years from early adulthood to midlife, as your wife also becomes a mother, you see her less as *Helen*, and more as *Eve*.

The danger comes at midlife, when your soul asks you to begin to transform your anima from the archetypal patterns of *Eve* to *Helen*, and then on to *Mary* and eventually *Sophia*.

Roberts puts it this way:

What happens in early adulthood in its classic form is that the two of you - husband and wife, mother and father - raise your children and start your careers. You are

---

[7] Roberts, William O., *In Crossing the Soul's River: A Right of Passage for Men*; The Pilgrim Press; Cleveland, OH; 1998

so busy that you have little time left over for psychological development.

But in midlife, that changes. And one of the first signs that it is changing is that the anima becomes activated deep in the male psyche. And when she does, she often puts new energy into the old adolescent conflict - the one between Eve (Mother) and Helen (Beauty). Men start flailing about to get some resolution to this conflict, and, too often they resolve it by projecting the undesired feminine onto their wives - she is experienced as a controlling mother - and the desired feminine onto the so-called "other woman "- she is bliss itself.

Of course the real *Eve* and *Helen* are patterns inside you. The women you fall in and out of love with as an adolescent, and the woman you eventually marry, are simply approximations of the internal Soul Mate. How else could "love at first sight" be explained? How could you fall in love with someone you don't even know, if not that they in some way match your internal template of the lover?

If you look outside yourself for *Helen*, and find her in another, usually younger, woman, you will likely have arrested your soul development, and be stuck halfway through the journey.

What you really need to do is go inward, using meditation, prayer, contemplation, therapy, spiritual counselling, fasting, or talking with other men (men's support groups are great for this), to discover your true Soul Mate, and after she transforms to *Helen*, keep the transformation going so over time she becomes *Mary*, the 'soul companion.'

This is demonstrated in the stage of marriage after the midlife transition, especially from the late 50s on, which is described as "companionable." The couple enjoys each other's company, shares in the daily chores of living, and takes turns leading and following in whatever activities they choose to do together.

With time, the Anima's transition to *Sophia*, the ancient Greek word meaning wisdom, is made, This, I believe is what leads us to become Elders, rather than simply elderly.

I feel as though I am now between the *Mary* and *Sophia* stages of my anima's transition. During my late forties and early fifties, thoughts of former girl friends frequently came unbidden into my mind. I wondered what these women were like now, and what it would have been like to marry them.

**An Exercise for
Encountering the Soul Mate**

Take a piece of paper and write the names of a number of women - maybe ten or twelve - to whom you are attracted. 'Identify the traits - physical and personal - that make each woman attractive. Review your list, looking for traits that are common among your attractions. What were your set of attractive traits five or ten years ago? How are your patterns of attraction changing? Finally, try to become conscious of how you respond when you find yourself attracted - and attractive - to these women. Do you become uneasy? Do you push them away? Or do you seek to draw them to you?

When he does this exercise with groups, Roberts says, "I am generally amazed at the response to this simple exercise. Men who rarely have the opportunity to think about their relationship with the feminine become aware of different notions of feminine attractiveness and of how those notions change as we mature."

Encountering the soul mate within seems to come more naturally as you grow spiritually, and become more authentically yourself. It is a gradual transition. After a while you look back and realize you are different now than you were a while ago.

But I also had enough life experience, especially having been widowed, divorced and now happily married again, to know that no matter how attractive a woman may seem in the beginning, the reality is that my romantic experience of the woman has more to do with me than her. In other words, as I withdrew my 'projection of perfection' from my partner, I experienced her more for who she was, rather than who I wanted her to be.

Soul Task Number Four: Speaking to Self

By now you are in the midst of the "soul's river", and at perhaps the most dangerous and challenging point in the journey. The danger is that, having struggled to get this far, you will turn and go back.

The whole task at midlife is to let go of your mask or persona – the image, or box you created for yourself to define who you are: accountant, family man, church leader, little league coach, whatever – and dive into the deep and unknown waters of the soul to find "the self."

The self

Whenever I think deeply on the nature of reality, and who I really 'am,' it doesn't take long before I realize that the 'little me' - the me I know through my "everyday ego consciousness" - is connected to a much larger reality. Carl Jung called it the self, which includes not only our ego consciousness, but also the unconscious psyche. The unconscious psyche is part and parcel of the Great Unknown, which we refer to as God, or The Creator, or the Higher Power, or a hundred other names.

So crossing the soul's river refers to the painful and confusing psychological and spiritual Odyssey where you let go of your
self-created persona, and connect with your true identity, which
is to be found in the Great Unknown. The payoff is a new, less
ego-centric energy that gives you new life and new purpose. It
leads you to your "true gifts," which you brought with you to
offer to the world.

In the Gnostic Gospel of Thomas, Jesus puts it this way: "If
you bring forth what is within you, what you bring forth will save
you. If you do not bring forth what is within you, what you do not
bring forth will destroy you."

Beware of Echo

In the Greek myth about Narcissus, the beautiful young lad
was out hunting when the nymph Echo spied him, and fell in love
with him. She could not hold her peace when others spoke, but
could not speak until others spoke first.

She followed Narcissus through the forest, and when he
sensed someone was there he called, "Is anyone here?" Echo
replied, "Here." Narcissus said, "Let us meet." She repeated, "Let
us meet," and ran to his arms. But Narcissus could not love her,
as he only loved himself.

The danger to midlife men is that the *Helen* you seek (Helen
is the beautiful feminine part of yourself that you project onto
other, usually younger, women) will be like Echo, adoring you,
echoing your every word, listening with rapt attention.

It is not hard to find an Echo, and even fall in love with her.
But you will learn nothing of value about your life or yourself
from her. And if you make the mistake of leaving your wife, who
may seem frumpy and familiar to you (though other men may
find her attractive), for this comely nymph, the illusion seldom

lasts long. Either your Echo, when the novelty of the relationship wears off, will stop hanging on your every word and begin to think for herself, or you will grow tired of the shallowness of the relationship.

Either that or you will remain shallow, and hurry back to the 'safe' bank of the river to rebuild your persona, and try to surround yourself with others, also insignificant, who will not challenge you.

As Roberts says in *Crossing the Soul's River,* "And this gets worse as we get older. We yearn for pretty, nubile, mindless Echo, a yes-woman who will delight with us as we stare at our reflection in the still water."

What you really need is to surround yourself with authentic people, who have gone on the journey themselves (this is the role of the Elder), and who will disturb your image in the still water, make you uncomfortable, and be with you as you dive down to find your deeper selves.

The Well of Grief

Those who will not slip beneath
the still surface of the well of grief

turning downward through its black water
to the place we cannot breathe

will never know the source from which we drink,
the secret water, cold and clear,

nor find in the darkness glimmering
the small, round coins
thrown by those who wished for something else.

~ David Whyte ~

Job, our Soul Brother

Many times, when I was in the midst of this struggle myself, I felt as though I was experiencing the trials of Job. It made me a little embarrassed to admit it, even to myself, as Job went through a lot tougher trials than I was experiencing, but the pattern felt similar.

As you recall, Job's life was going along swimmingly - beautiful children, lovely wife, great wealth - and he was a devout and righteous man. In other words, he had everything in order, and lived the way he was "supposed" to live. Then God and Satan are having a chat, and God starts to brag about how devout Job is. Satan says, "Let me have a go at him, I bet I can make him mad at you."

God says, in effect, "Ok, have a go. Just don't kill him."

Job didn't know what hit him. All of a sudden he lost it all, through no fault of his own. His three friends came along, and tried to make him "go back across the soul's river."

"Go on back home and start over," one says.

"You must have screwed up somehow," says another. "Stay with me a while and we will see if we can straighten you out."

"Give up," says the third, "There is nothing you can do."

But Job hangs in there. He stays the course, seeking the truth. In the end, he hears a voice in a whirlwind questioning him:

Who is this that darkens counsel
By words without knowledge?
Gird up your loins like a man,
I will question you, and you shall declare to me.
Where were you when I laid the foundation of the earth?
Tell me, if you have understanding.
Who determined its measurements? Surely you know!
Who stretched the line upon it? (Job 38: 1-5)

Now here is the interesting thing: similar words to these are found in Proverbs, in a section that describes Sophia, feminine wisdom:

Ages ago I was set up,
*   at the first, before the beginning of the earth...*
When he marked out the foundations of the earth
*   then I was beside him, like a master workman,*
and I was daily his delight,
*   rejoicing before him always*
rejoicing in his inhabited world
*   and delighting in the sons of men. (Proverbs 8:23, 29-30)*

Aha! Job has taken feminine wisdom into his soul, and is ready to live life "according to the program of the second half," as Jung said.

I noticed, as I went through my own "trials of Job:" financial meltdown, loss of energy and focus, mild depression, loss of libido, confusion about my life mission, and loss of confidence, that I could feel my feminine self starting to emerge. It now feels as though the masculine and feminine energies are balanced within me. I also have the energy back that I had in my forties, but now it is more thoughtful and less egocentric. I have even recovered from the financial losses of my fifties.

I feel more in tune with the Higher Power as well.

So that is the journey. It begins when things start to break down. You lose interest in what you used to be passionate about, you become dissatisfied with your life and long for something different. You feel empty, or dead inside.

You then encounter your shadow, which, if you have the courage to own it, can lead you to your wounds, which can lead you to your gold.

You must also discover your Soul Mate – the feminine within you, and not project her onto the women in your life.

Then, like Job, you hang in there, persistently seeking the truth about Who You Are, and incorporating all those parts of you disowned by you over the years.

The danger is you will quit somewhere along the way, and "go back home." But the rewards for making it all the way across are great. You will feel a sense of purpose, peace, well-being, energy and love. Then you can be there for the others who are struggling on their own crossings.

Shift Gears in Midlife

Three Steps to Spiritual Growth

There are two periods in our lives when we ask the 'Big Questions': puberty (remember those terrible, exciting, confusing teenage years?) and midlife. We ask: What is my life about? Is there life after death, and if so what do I need to do to prepare for it? What is the nature of God? How do I establish a spiritual life? I am not saying we don't ask these questions at other stages of life, but during these two periods, in my observation and experience, these questions arise somewhat unbidden.

In your teen years you were passionate about things, and you explored ideas about life, God and the opposite sex. And of course tried to figure out who you were, because every day when you looked in the mirror, a different person seemed to be peering back at you, with a bigger nose, or ears, or a bit more facial hair than the fellow the day before. And you didn't know quite what was going on. "What you wanted to be when you grew up" changed every few months, until finally you "grew up and got a job."

Well, some things never change! After a few decades during which you may have married (and maybe re-married), established a career, raised kids, bought a house and did all the other things typical of the "busy years," midlife brings you right back to the Big Questions: What is the meaning of my life? What is the nature of God (or whatever name you choose for the All-That-Is)? How does one grow spiritually?

By "spiritual" I mean the unseen. Those forces at work in your lives that you experience yet can't get in touch with through your five senses. Those forces the mystics throughout the ages have talked about, and that breakthroughs in leading-edge physics are beginning to reveal. These unseen forces seem mysterious to you because you can't see, touch, taste or smell them, but you can feel their effects. Spiritual growth helps you adapt to and even use these forces to your advantage for living life more fully, with a greater sense of joy and well-being.

There are many Hero Journey folktales. Joseph Campbell describes the hero as "someone who has given his life to something bigger than himself," and that is an accurate description of the spiritual journey as well. In fact, the Hero's Journey is a perfect metaphor for the journey of spiritual growth.

The hero may set out intentionally, like Beowulf or Sir Gawain, or may be thrown into the adventure. Like the hero, you are either called to the spiritual journey through inner urgings, or thrown into it through a crisis of some kind. In my case, I was always interested in the concept of God and life after death, but the event that threw me into a far more active search – started me on the journey, so to speak – was the car accident that killed my first wife. It was ten years before I had a "spiritual awakening," but I was "journeying" all the time, trying to figure things out.

My research and experience suggests there are three Keys to finding the answers:

- Intention
- Action
- Surrender

Intention, the First Step to Spiritual Growth

The process is simple, but not easy (isn't that the way it is with most worthwhile endeavours?), and it begins with Intention. In fact, everything we do in life, from picking up our fork at the dinner table, to starting a major business project, begins with intention. Spiritual growth is no different. It begins with the simple intention to increase our spiritual awareness. Desire is another word for it. We must want to increase our spiritual awareness before anything else happens.

Here's an example.

Twenty five years ago I asked some friends, who seemed to have a kind of happiness I didn't have, how they got it. They told me to come to their evangelical church and give my life to Jesus. I was already an elder in a different church, and didn't want to switch, but I did want what they had (Intention, Desire).

Action Is the Second Key to Spiritual Growth

I began to pray to be made ready for what they had (Action) and when I was ready, it was given to me. Eventually I was led to

Alcoholics Anonymous, where by doing the Steps (Action), I had a spiritual awakening, and lost all craving for alcohol.

It is a universal law that whatever you intend begins coming toward you. That doesn't mean you just sit there and wait. God will work with you not for you.

If you want to increase your spiritual awareness simply be clear about what you intend, and then get into action (start reading books on spiritual development, join a group, try praying or meditating). As you take action, you will receive the guidance you need. It could come as a chance meeting with someone who can help, or some other serendipitous event, but it will happen. Your intention and action lead you to the answers you need. They may not be the ones you want to hear, but they are the best ones for this time in your life. Open yourself. Surrender.

Surrender Is the Third Key to Spiritual Growth

Now, surrender is a scary word to most folks. It implies giving up power, losing control, being vulnerable. In fact your ego will throw up all kinds of scary scenarios to keep you from surrendering to something Higher. The ego, which believes it is in control (and is, until you surrender), fears its annihilation.

These scary scenarios can be powerful, and each ego knows just the story its 'owner' (i.e. you) needs to hear to keep you from surrendering. For one person, it is the fear of losing a loved one; for another, it is the fear of having to let go of a favourite pastime. For me it was the fear that if I surrendered my life to a Higher Power (God), He would send me to help out in some remote village in Africa, and my family wouldn't come, and I'd lose them, but I'd have to go anyway. I know that sounds weird, but to me it was real. Your ego knows just the scary story to tell to keep you from taking the Big Step.

A Room in Tibet

There is a story about a room somewhere in Tibet, where once every one hundred years a person walking through would become enlightened. Before the person enters the room, he or she is given two pieces of advice: "All is not as it seems." And "Keep your feet moving". The person then enters the room, the door is closed, and the person is faced with ... his fears! If he can manage not to be paralyzed by his fears (all is not as it seems) and keep his feet moving, he can reach the door on the other side, and emerge enlightened.

The first time I heard that story I thought it would be pretty neat to go through that room. Just think, walk through a room and presto: enlightenment. How hard could it be? After all, a person's fears aren't real. What you meet in the room is just illusions.

But as I thought about it I realized I let fears hold me back in real life all the time. What would be the difference if I were facing them in a room? The challenge is the same. Letting go of fear is a spiritual endeavour, and surrender is one of the big keys.

It does not matter how you go about surrendering. Evangelical churches encourage their members to come to the altar and give their lives to Jesus. The approach in Twelve Step Programs is to, "Turn your life and your will over to the care of God as you understand him." Other spiritual teachings have still other approaches, but in every one, the eventual goal is to surrender one's ego self to a Higher Power, whatever name that Power is given.

As I have mentioned, I came at it through Alcoholics Anonymous, and was desperate enough that I finally overcame my ego fear and turned my life over to the care of God as I understood Him. The result was nothing like what my ego feared. Rather than being sent to Africa, I was filled with love and joy where there had been fear and anxiety. I experienced a Peace I could not have imagined existing. I was given the certain knowledge that the Higher Power (God) loves me unconditionally.

I also lost my fear of death, and a bunch of other fears that hindered my life. Although I am not fearless now (I still have fears that hold me back somewhat), I have WAY less fear than I used to.

All it took was total, unconditional surrender, which of course is the most fearful thing we humans can imagine!

If you want to give it a try, you can pray fervently and surrender all at once, or just surrender a little every day. It doesn't matter. Just keep your feet moving, and you will find yourself gaining enlightenment as you go.

When a Transition Becomes a Crisis

Daniel Levinson, in his book *The Seasons of a Man's Life*, says we go through a transition about every ten years, and each ten-year "epoch" entails certain tasks. Levinson labels age 40-45 the "midlife transition," and says it is often a crisis. Here is a quote from his book re: the midlife transition...

> Every life structure necessarily gives high priority to certain aspects of the self and neglects or minimizes other aspects. This is as true of the Settling Down structure of the Thirties as of all others.
>
> In the Mid-life Transition these neglected parts of the self urgently seek expression. A man experiences them as "other voices in other rooms" (in Truman Capote's evocative phrase). Internal voices that have been muted for years now clamour to be heard. At times they are heard

as a vague whispering, the content unclear but the tone indicating grief over lost opportunities, outrage over betrayal by others, or guilt over betrayal by oneself.

At other times they come through as a thunderous roar, the content all too clear, stating names and times and places and demanding that something be done to right the balance.

A man hears the voice of an identity prematurely rejected; of a love lost or not pursued; of a valued interest or relationship given up in acquiescence to parental or other authority; of an internal figure who wants to be an athlete or nomad or artist, to marry for love or remain a bachelor, to get rich or enter the clergy or live a sensual carefree life - possibilities set aside earlier to become what he now is.

During the Mid-life Transition he must learn to listen more attentively to these voices and decide consciously what part he will give them in his life.

I believe that almost all men go through a major change or transition (which could feel like a crisis) at some point. You may wonder if you're "supposed" to be in crisis. Although middle aged and undergoing some changes, you don't feel like things are that bad. Or you may be in your sixties or even seventies, and still waiting for your midlife crisis. But it may not happen at midlife.

For example a man in his late twenties or early thirties, who has not settled into a career and/or marriage during his twenties, may feel as though he is in crisis in his early thirties, as he tries to figure out what to do. He may feel as though he is falling behind his peers, or perhaps is getting not-so-subtle pressure from his parents suggesting it is time to decide on something and "get going". Having gone through a crisis in his thirties, such a man may barely notice his midlife transition at 40-45 years.

By forty I had already tried oil patch work, cross-cultural adult education, guiding and outfitting, direct marketing, and television journalism, and none of them seemed to be 'it,' although I learned a lot with each of them. I had the urgent feeling that I had better figure out what my "right livelihood" was! At a church retreat I had a very powerful 'vision experience' where I was shown what appeared to be the Soul of the Earth. It is difficult to describe this experience, but it was as though I could see this entity with my eyes and in my mind. It was a beautiful emerald-coloured Presence, powerful and yet vulnerable, and I realized in the moment of this vision that we humans were abusing it. I decided as a result of this experience that my mission would be to spend the rest of my life helping people take better care of the earth.

Acting on this mission, I had within two years quit my job, gone back to university, left my dysfunctional marriage, and established a new, and very fulfilling relationship with Elizabeth, who is now my wife of 20 years. Everything felt good and exciting. None felt like a crisis, but it had all the markings of what Levinson describes.

My fifties though, were a different matter. I entered a long period where I was aware I was going through a major transition at a very deep level, and there did not seem to be anything I could do to hasten it. It felt as though it was to a large degree a spiritual transition, where my very being was changing in some way. Now, at age 64, I have as much energy as I did in my forties, but it is 'deepened' in a way that is hard to describe. I feel wiser, and more able to sort out the important from the inconsequential.

How about you? What other voices in other rooms are you hearing? Are they vague whisperings or a thunderous roar? What can you do within your current life structure to respond? You may begin a new hobby or take a course in communication so you can talk at a deeper level with your wife or partner about your longings and dreams. Whether you choose a new direction or continue as you are, pay more attention to your spiritual development. Whether you strengthen it through church, prayer, meditation, coaching or retreats it will help tremendously when you are in crisis.

A Time of Quest

Possibly you've avoided a crisis at mid-life but you will still go through a transition. This is often seen by researchers as a time of quest. It can be a quest for wholeness, a quest for integrity, a quest for love, a quest for independence as well as interdependence, or a quest for the sacred. It can be a time for the healing of old wounds or for finding one's true calling.

Psychologist Carl Jung believed that in the second half of life people begin to discover and express qualities in themselves that were underdeveloped or neglected in the first half and in doing so they achieve wholeness and balance.

Midlife may also bring a re-evaluation of relationships and a search for deeper intimacy. This happens to both men and women at this stage. You want to free yourself from sex-role limitations and allow both the "masculine" and "feminine" in yourself to merge.

If you haven't figured out "what you are going to do when you grow up," this midlife transition will be a time of pondering your right livelihood. Few people know what kind of work will be truly fulfilling when they are teenagers, or in their early twenties. As Joseph Campbell used to say, we climb the corporate ladder only to find it is leaning against the wrong wall.

Many men and women in 'promising' careers completely change direction at midlife and even though they may take a big cut in pay, find life as an elementary school teacher, or even a construction crew worker more satisfying than being a stock broker or high-powered executive.

Perhaps one of the most important aspects of a midlife transition is the quest for the sacred. As a child you may have had spiritual instruction in a church, temple, mosque or synagogue, but as you become an adult, the childhood ideas of God seem too, well... childish. Like many, you may have become so busy that you simply let the spiritual aspect of your life atrophy.

At midlife, the big questions about the meaning of life come back unbidden. Perhaps they are triggered by the death of someone you are close to, or by a serious accident or illness. However they come, they get your attention and you start a search for meaning at a deeper level. You may go back to formal religion, or you may seek it on your own through prayer, meditation, retreats, or other spiritual disciplines.

Now... anyone can "refuse the call," and choose not to change as they go through this time. In the hero's journey folktales, if a person gets the call to adventure, but refuses to answer, and just goes back to his daily life in the village, there is no adventure, and the protagonist simply lives his life out in the village, never knowing what special boon he could have brought to the community.

So... if you are feeling the call to adventure in the form of internal urgings to examine your livelihood, or your relationships, or your understanding of the meaning of life, answer the call. It may not lead to a crisis, but it will surely lead to a more fulfilling life!

As Robert Atkinson, Associate Professor of Human Development at the University of Southern Maine says, "It is in the second half of life that people discover what is personally sacred-what matters to them most in this life and beyond. Learning what that is may be the greatest midlife challenge of all."

No Longer This, But Not Yet That

The move into the second half of life, or what in France is called the "third life," doesn't happen overnight, as you have probably noticed. It is a transition, and transitions take time. Transitions have another feature that is no fun to experience. They are periods of "nothingness," when we are no longer what we used to be, but not yet what we are becoming.

Martin Buber puts it this way:

Nothing in the world can change from one reality into another, unless it first turns into nothing, that is, into the reality of the between-stage. In that stage it is nothing, and no one can grasp it, for it has reached the rung of nothingness, just as before creation. And then it is made into a new creature, from the egg to the chick. The moment when the egg is no more, and the chick is not yet, is nothingness.[8]

Perhaps you feel as though you are in a stage of "nothingness," where you no longer feel interest in things you used to be passionate about, and wonder if anything can turn you on. Maybe

---

[8] The Maggid of Mezritch; Martin Buber; from "Tales of the Hasidim"; P.104.

you feel as though you are just "spinning your wheels" or "putting in time," and that your life has lost its "juice." The chances are good that you are in a midlife transition.

I spent about five years in a midlife transition during my early fifties, and it was no fun. But I had enough life experience by that time to know that everything in life eventually passes - the good and the bad. As that old Roger Miller song said, "The good ain't forever, and the bad ain't for good."

Transitions have three stages: Leaving the last existence, being in 'limbo' or 'nothingness', and then entering the new existence.

When one is in the middle stage – nothingness – it is the time to look for slight hints of what is to come next. Robert A. Johnson, in his book *Balancing Heaven And Earth* (Harper Collins, 1998) calls it "following the slender threads," where you look for any little thing that catches your attention, makes your heart beat a little faster, or perhaps gives you a small rush of energy. It is difficult to find these slender threads, but if one keeps looking, they will appear. You might pick up the end of a thread at a chance meeting with someone who is doing work you have always thought might be interesting, but have discounted because there "wasn't any money in it," or it "wasn't practical."

Perhaps you will find a slender thread through volunteering with some organization that seems to you worthwhile. Maybe it will be through your church, or through a men's organization, such as The ManKind Project.

Transition, though confusing, and depressing at times, is also a time pregnant with promise. You are no longer what you used to be, and you are not yet what you are becoming, so you can be or do anything!

In my experience, going through transitions requires patience, and "active waiting." In other words, keep exploring new possibilities. Try new things. Don't just sit and wait for inspiration to come. As the saying goes, "God will work with you, not for you."

And remember - this too shall pass.

The Ozymandias Complex

When you are a young man, you often have a big dream such as becoming the president of the company, building a successful business, becoming a well-know actor. What you don't recognize is that along with this dream you subconsciously believe that success means your life will be great in all kinds of other ways (e.g., wealth will also bring fame, intelligence, a great sex life, and happiness). It is a grandiose dream – your personal myth – wherein you are the hero engaged in a noble quest.

Sometimes a man achieves his dream, and becomes a bit insufferable, thinking he knows more than he does about all kinds of things. I have heard it described as "a self-made man, in love with his maker." I call this the Ozymandias Complex after the poem by Shelley, and I think we all have it to a degree.

Shelley's poem was actually referring to Pharaoh Ramses II, the greatest of all the ancient Pharaohs (both in what he did, and in his own mind). He lived to be 92 years old, and ruled Egypt for 67 years (1279 B.C. to 1212 B.C.). Ozymandias is apparently a Greek derivation of one his many Egyptian names, User-maat-re.

Here is a quote from one of Ramses's statues: "I am Ozymandias, King of Kings. If anyone would know how great I am and where I lie, let him surpass any of my works."

And here is Shelley's poem (in case you forgot it):

Ozymandias

I met a traveler from an antique land
Who said: Two vast and trunkless legs of stone
Stand in the desert. Near them, on the sand,
Half sunk, a shattered visage lies, whose frown,
And wrinkled lip, and sneer of cold command,
Tell that its sculptor well those passions read,
Which yet survive, stamped on these lifeless things,
The hand that mocked them, and the heart that fed,
And on the pedestal these words appear:
"My name is Ozymandias, King of Kings:
Look upon my works, ye Mighty, and despair!"
Nothing beside remains. Round the decay
Of that colossal wreck, boundless and bare
The lone and level sands stretch far away.

-Percy Bysshe Shelley
1792-1822

Getting Over the Ozymandias Complex

Along comes midlife and whacks you on the head. You realize your dream was largely an illusion, and you discover that even if you are successful in a business or profession, you won't live happily ever after.

It can be quite a shock, and can lead to a midlife crisis. The stronger you held the dream, and the greater your early success, the bigger the shock to discover it was an illusion.

One of the tasks at midlife is to recognize that the assumptions that go with the big dream were made by a youth, and were incorrect. True happiness comes from recognizing 'what is,' accepting things that cannot be changed, and making the inner journey to discover your connection with the Divine - or greater Reality.

The danger is that you will look outside for what can only be found inside. It shows up in all the stereotypical behaviours - quitting a job, leaving a wife, getting a young girlfriend, getting your hair dyed, getting a sporty little car.

How do you let go of your Ozymandias Complex? I think the first step is to recognize that things didn't turn out the way you thought, and then accept that your life is okay anyway. Then you begin the inner journey. Personal growth workshops, meditation, prayer, and the *New Warrior Adventure Training* (www.mankindproject.org) are all good ways to begin. My e-book, *Picking up the Burning Feather* (www.midlife-men.com/spirituality.html) can be a guide as well.

Feelings on the Rise

In midlife, it is common for men to become more emotional. You may feel little emotion for years and suddenly feel yourself moved to tears at movies, or find a lump in their throat when thinking about your children or grandchildren, or even the condition of the earth.

You might find this distressing. You don't want to appear weak in front of your peers. And that's understandable.

But there are benefits. While many things can lead to a feeling of dissatisfaction with life, a key to feeling satisfied is knowing what you are feeling, and being able to express it.

I know, I know, "getting in touch with your feelings" sounds like a cliché and touchy-feely. But in my experience, very little contributes as much to a feeling of satisfaction with life as knowing what you are feeling, and being able to share your feelings with another human being, especially your wife/partner. NOTHING increases intimacy as much as sharing your feelings with the one you love.

Ok, you say, but I don't even know what I am feeling half the time.

Fair enough. My observation is that men are socialized when young to have a narrow range of feelings: anger, resentment, love (i.e. feeling horny), and maybe happiness (i.e. when our team wins a game). Men are specifically conditioned NOT to recognize, and especially not ADMIT to feeling hurt, fear (except maybe fear of physical pain), anxiety, loneliness or any other "weak" emotion. It isn't that men don't have all the other feelings, they just aren't aware of them.

I am generalizing here, but I am not far off. Some research shows that by the time boys are two years old they are already being conditioned to tune out their feelings, while girls are about thirteen before this starts happening to them.

About 35 years ago I went to a time management workshop based on Transactional Analysis, to learn how to know what I felt. It was difficult at first. So many of the feelings men have are lumped under the heading of Anger, or "feeling low" (i.e. depression, which is rampant among men). I learned a process to identify and assess my feelings at any given time (see Section One: Fine-Tuning the Mind; Midlife Transitions; What on Earth am I Feeling?), and then have the courage to share them.

That step was the hardest... admitting to my wife (or whoever I had the feeling about) what I was feeling, especially if it was anger or resentment about some "small" thing that had been said or done. I was afraid I would appear petty, and the person would not want to be with me any more.

Of course the results of speaking my true feelings were always the opposite of what I feared, but it took a while to trust the process. Plus, I had to be sure not to blame the person I was having the feeling about (usually my wife), or point fingers at her for "making me feel bad", so I had to learn how to use "I"statements (See Section One: Fine-Tuning The Mind; Midlife Transitions; The Power of "I").

Now I pretty much know what I am feeling at any moment, and if I don't I can tune in quickly and find out. The payoff in increased intimacy and satisfaction with my life is immeasurable.

Maybe you feel it's not manly to share your feelings. Let me share with you part of a note I received from a female friend a while back:

> I was struck by something my former husband said to me a couple of months ago. Our nine-year-old daughter is struggling with getting her emotional needs met at school and with dad. Her teacher gave us some things to work on with her and I told him about it. I told him that to support our daughter, her teacher asked us to work with her more to ask her how she feels, what she wants, what's missing and to encourage her to ask for what she wants.

> My ex-husband said, "Well you know I have a hard time with feelings." So that's not going to happen here. I was very sad for both him and our daughter. There's a whole chasm between him and his daughter which is so vital to what women want in a loving relationship: to simply feel heard and validated.

> With our six year old son, I kiss him goodbye when they leave to go with dad. He told me that our son didn't like to be kissed anymore, that big boys don't kiss. Again - from a female point of view only - I think this may be common and it would be an amazing gift to men in the

world if they could feel safe and free to experience and express their full range of emotions- in a male way.

Being uncomfortable with feelings might be macho (although I am not sure of that), but it is certainly not manly. In fact in traditional societies, the fiercest warrior is not afraid to show love, compassion, or other "soft" emotions.

This inability to recognize and/or express our whole range of feelings robs us of a great deal of love, pleasure, joy and satisfaction in life. For one thing, it keeps us from telling people we love that we love them.

I see this over and over with men who have lost their fathers, and wish they had told their dads that they loved them. And also wished their dads had told them the same thing! I've also met men who were estranged from sons, daughters or other family members. They have so much fear about appearing vulnerable, that they just can't say what the other is longing to hear. If that's manly, I want no part of it.

The movie *8 Seconds* is about a world champion bull rider who gets killed by a bull. For years he has striven to gain his father's love and recognition, but his dad is too afraid to express any deep emotion. In the early morning after his son is killed, his wife finds the father sitting in the living room, trying to remember whether he ever told his son he loved him.

So, if you want to increase your satisfaction with life, a BIG STEP is learning how to feel your feelings, and talk openly about them. You'll live longer if you do.

Getting Past Our Foolishness

Earth Elder was Alexander Wolfe's grandfather, an Anishnaybay Indian who lived in western Canada and died in 1937 at age 106.

He was alive during the period when European settlers came into the Canadian prairies. In *Earth Elder Stories*[9], we read about his family and the Anishnaybay culture during his lifetime.

One thing Earth Elder told his grandson caught my eye, and I thought it nicely describes the transition we are faced with at midlife. Here is the quote from Earth Elder:

> There is a period in the life of every person in which there is foolishness. When this period passes some people will grow up remembering and using what they there told. For this we have a saying, 'When you have had enough foolishness, then you become knowledgeable and know your mistakes.' There are others who never go beyond this first stage; they remain foolish for the rest of their lives. To those people we say, "Your foolishness will accompany you to your old age."

One of the gifts I found when I reached midlife was to be able to look back at things I used to think were incredibly important and say, "What was all that about?" I could also look back at people I had hurt, or the things I felt embarrassed about having done, and make amends to the people, and forgive myself for my foolishness. I could also take the lessons from each 'foolish' circumstance, and gain a bit of wisdom.

This is not to say I no longer do any foolish things! I do them fairly regularly, but they are a "higher grade" of foolishness.

I have met a fair number of men who have not gone beyond the first stage. They continue making impulsive, or self-destructive decisions, fishtailing all over the place. They continue

---

9 Wolfe, Alexander; *Earth Elder Stories*; Wolfe, Alexander; Fifth House Publishing; Saskatoon, Saskatchewan; 1988.

to think their happiness depends on how others around them treat them. They feel victimized and blame others for whatever bad happens in their lives. They refuse to take responsibility for themselves. In other words, they have not had enough foolishness yet! When these men get old, they become bitter, and still blame the world for not treating them better.

What about you? Have you had enough foolishness? Can you take the lessons from your past foibles, accept responsibility for them, learn from them, forgive yourself and move on with more wisdom? Yes? Good. You no longer delight in playing the fool. May you grow to be wise and compassionate as you learn from any foolishness that follows.

Find and Feed Your Passion

These tips come from the Rachel Green newsletter (www.rachelgreen.com). Ms. Green is a speaker and coach from Australia. Her suggestions are especially meaningful in midlife. Here they are:

Midlife is about what's important, about following your passion, about following your dreams. So here are 10 tips on how to find your passion.

What are your strengths?
Write down what your strengths are. Are you using them?

Advertise Yourself:
Write an advert on yourself for a personal column. All those glowing adjectives about yourself - are they obvious in the way you live your life at the moment?

Notice what you do in life:
Monitor the things you do in your life, and notice which things leave you feeling good about yourself and which leave you drained or down. Work out ways to do more of the former and less of the latter.

If you won the Lotto:
Ask yourself - if I won the Lotto tomorrow what would I do differently in my life? Now find ways to do it without winning.

Happiness:
Ask yourself - what would really make me happy? Find ways to do it.

Do the important things:
Ask yourself - if you only had 2 more years to live, what would you most want to do? Find ways to do it now. Don't keep putting the important things off.

Keep a list:
Ask your friends and family what things they think you're really good at. Keep a list. Then look at your life and work out whether you are using your strengths and if not, work out how to.

Hold onto your dreams:
What did you always dream of doing as a child, around the age of six or seven? Have you done those things? If not, can you still do them?

Values:

What values did you support as a teenager - were you active in a political party, a social group, in wanting to do voluntary service overseas - what? Did you continue to support those values? If not, would they still be important now?

How do you want to be remembered?

Decide what you'd like your epitaph to say and make sure your life allows that to happen!

Be passionate, have a purpose, do what's important and happiness will come to you.

The Sunset & Beyond

Choosing Happiness

I used to think my happiness depended upon other people – my wife, my boss, the circumstances of my life. I spent a lot of my time feeling anxious, resentful and angry. Why couldn't the people around me just treat me right, so I could feel happy? I remember reading personal growth books, and popular psychology books, which suggested we create our own reality, but I was sure that was not true for me.

When I joined AA and did the steps, I ended up having a profound spiritual awakening, and with it came the realization that I had, indeed, been running my own life, and creating my own reality all along! I finally understood that my happiness did depend on me. How I saw and interpreted the world around me depended on my internal state of being. "As inside, so outside."

Here is a quote from Courtney Milne's website and his wonderful, daily *Pool of Possibilities* (www.poolofpossibilities.com) May 22, 2008:

> Being here at the pool today makes me happy. There just is not a better way of expressing my joy of the moment. I am happy because the water is mirroring such vivid colours and the trees are so verdant. But this is a mere surface description of the deeper story. The truth is, I create the happiness, and the pool reflects what is already within me. Just like this image of trees and clouds, the idea that the pool 'makes' me happy is an illusion. My observation is that most people most of the time acquire their happiness from circumstances that fluctuate from moment to moment, thus their happiness is always short-lived.

> If, instead, we realize that happiness is a choice, we can easily be happy throughout virtually all of our waking day. In her book, *Happy for No Reason*, Marci Shimoff[10] says when we no longer rely on our surroundings to be happy our souls can be nurtured anytime. We don't have to wait for a reason.

It is common at midlife to go through periods of discontent, depression, irritability and unhappiness. If you don't realize your world is a reflection of your inner life, you can end up casting about for someone to blame. If you are at that stage, know that

---

[10] Shimoff, Marci; Happy For No Reason:7 Steps to Being Happy from the Inside Out;Free Press; New York, NY; 2008.

"this too shall pass," and try looking inward for the cause of your pain, and the possible source of peace, contentment and happiness. Prayer, meditation, psychological counselling, and even Marci Shimoff's book can all be helpful.

Following the Slender Threads

Chances are you have had an experience that follows a pattern something like this: You are going on a trip, have made the plans carefully, and have your itinerary figured out. You set off, full of confidence, and then things start to go wrong. You miss a flight, or a train or bus, and have to spend an extra day somewhere not on your itinerary. But while you are being 'inconvenienced,' you meet an interesting person who is doing work you have always thought would be great to do, and the person is looking to hire someone!

I think we all experience this kind of pattern in our lives at one time or other. Jungian psychologist Robert A. Johnson, in his book *Balancing Heaven and Earth* calls it following the slender threads. Here is what he says about it (p.99-101):

> The concept of listening to the will of God is difficult for many modern people to follow, as it collides with our love of freedom and our insistence on free will. However, I must declare that, with respect to the most important aspects of my life, I am not free. I am safest when I let go of trying to control my life and instead follow the slender threads. This is a religious perspective in the sense that the human ego must surrender to something more powerful than itself.
>
> Freedom insists that the ego can do anything it wishes. I do not mean to toss the concept of freedom out entirely.

Of course we have free will, but I am insisting that in every moment there is one right thing to do: we can choose to follow the will of God or not follow the will of God, and only in this way can we live meaningful lives.

I have learned to trust the slender threads for the big decisions in my life while using my ego to take care of the small details. I thought I was free when I willed my way onto a ship to Europe, but my plan soon broke under me. The concept of freedom can become an inflation. When my inflationary bubble burst, the slender threads in all their power continued to function and guide me in a particular way, connecting me with Art Meyer and ultimately taking me to Dr. Jung's study....

... How do we know if we are truly following the will of God? One knows instinctively; there is a sense of peace, balance and fullness, and unhurriedness.

When I joined AA I not only got sober and had a profound spiritual awakening, but I began to realize that there was a Higher Power (God as we understand Him), who was far more capable of guiding me than my ego was.

It was through following the slender threads (being open to guidance, chance encounters, and other 'coincidences' in my life) that I ended up at a church retreat that helped me find my mission in life.

The slender threads also led me to a chance meeting with a fellow Elizabeth and I partnered with to develop a device for harvesting water out of the air. It was a bad investment from a financial point of view (we lost our money), but it was good in that it led us to live in Vancouver for five years while we both went through major midlife transitions.

The midlife transition led me to build the midlife-men web-site, and start a newsletter. Possibly, something in it became a slender thread for you to follow.

This is a time in your life to become aware of the "chance en-counters" that offer new possibilities and follow them up. Don't simply carry on with your life, telling yourself the direction the slender threads would take you isn't practical or that it is just a coincidence and doesn't mean a thing.

Heal Yourself: Give

In my conversations with midlife men, I find many interested in mentoring younger people, or volunteering their time to good causes. I think this is a normal desire as you get older, and it turns out it is also a healthy thing to do.

Here is an excerpt from *The Lark Letter: A woman's Guide to Optimal Health & Balance* (www.drlark.com), the April, 2004 edition. I found it interesting and thought you might too.

The philosopher Plato spent much time teaching his stu-dents that there was no healing of the body without sim-ultaneous healing of the mind. Today we have psychoneuroimmunology, a fancy word for a field of study created in the 1970s to address the growing awareness in medicine that your physical, mental, emo-tional, and spiritual health are inextricably intertwined.

In modern times, thousands of studies have been done, which give scientific validity to the age-old wisdom that what you do with your mind and emotions has a power-ful effect on your health.

Harvard researchers studied the effects of altruism by taking before-and-after measurements of immune system markers in the saliva of volunteers who watched three films: the first on gardening, the second about the Nazis, and the third about Mother Teresa. There was no change in immune markers before or after the first two films, but after the third one, a marker for improved immune function rose dramatically. In other words, just watching someone else be generous is good for your health.

In another landmark study, a researcher from the University of Michigan followed 2,700 people for more than a decade to determine how their social relationships affected their health. He found that more than any other activity, doing volunteer work improved health and increased life expectancy.

Psychologists Allan Luks and Howard Andrews collected surveys from more than 3,000 student volunteers and found that their "helper's high" was followed by a second stage they called the "healthy-helper syndrome." They defined this stage as "a longer-lasting sense of calm and heightened emotional well-being ... that is a powerful antidote to stress, a key to happiness and optimism, and a way to combat feelings of helplessness and depression."

The Danger of the Older Man Syndrome

Perhaps you have noticed, as I have, that as we age we acquire an unpleasant habit of having opinions on all kinds of things, and feel that our opinions must be heard. I have noticed this in my Dad's generation, and do not find it endearing! Often you may want to tell this older person to put a lid on it, and hopefully you find the patience to "be still".

Here, in "An Older Man's Letter to God," one man addresses that very thing:

Dear Lord,

You know better than I know myself that I am growing older and will some day be old. Keep me from the fatal habit of thinking that I must say something on every subject and on every occasion.

Release me from craving to straighten out everybody's affairs. Make me thoughtful but not moody; helpful but not bossy.

With my vast store of wisdom, it seems a pity not to use it all, but you know Lord that I want a few friends at the end.

Keep my mind free from the recital of endless details; give me wings to get to the point.

Seal my lips on my aches and pains...they are increasing, and love of rehearsing them is becoming sweeter as the years go by.

I dare not ask for grace enough to enjoy the tales of other's pains, but to help me endure them with patience.

I dare not ask for improved memory, but for a growing humility and a lessening cocksureness when my memory seems to clash with the memories of others.

Teach me the glorious lesson that occasionally I may be mistaken.

Keep me reasonably sweet; I do not want to be a Saint - some of them are so hard to live with - but a sour old person is one of the crowning works of evil.

Give me the ability to see good things in unexpected people...and give me, O Lord, the grace to tell them so.

AMEN

I first saw it in the April, 2004 edition of Harper's Magazine. It is taken from the Spiritual Letters section of LibraryOnline Inc., a website that provides hundreds of letter templates that can be modified online and then printed or emailed to friends and colleagues.

Power up Your Life

In her book *The Dynamic Laws of Healing*, Catherine Ponder talks about the hidden or secret power of the phrase "I AM". She writes, "There are strange powers lying dormant within that name. All that you dream of as desirable can be released through the redeeming words 'I AM', because these words stir up the divine nature within you. 'I AM' is the name of God within you."

If you are familiar with the Old Testament, you will recall that when Moses went up the mountain and received the Ten Commandments, he asked who he should say he had been talking to. God said to tell them it was I AM.

I have a friend who works with groups of all kinds to reduce conflict and reach consensus on important issues. He says when you are suffering a trauma, such as a separation, it is a useful idea to start off with a statement that describes why you are sad, or angry, or whatever. For example, "I am hurt because (Jenny) left me." Then take off the reason you are hurt: "I am hurt." Then take off the feeling, and you are left with "I am", and it gives you a feeling of wholeness that makes the hurt less hurtful.

Here is a meditation I suggest you try:

For five minutes each day, quiet your mind, and repeat "I AM" either out loud, or to yourself. Do this every day for a week, and see how you feel.

I have been doing this for a while now and am impressed with the results. I feel more energized, focussed, and more positive. Of course you do not need to stop this exercise after a week! It's just that you should do it regularly for a week in order to begin feeling the benefits.

After five minutes of repeating I AM, you can add things such as "I am healthy," "I am prosperous," "I am peaceful," or whatever else you want to add that you desire in your life.

Do not add negative statements, such as "I am lonely," or "I am angry," as these statements also have power.

Pay attention to the words you inadvertently attach to the "I AM" handle of power. If you find yourself saying "I AM always too busy," try changing it to "I am filled with energy and joy to accomplish my work quickly and easily."

Remember, there is power in words. Use this meditation wisely.

The Lesson of the Labyrinth

Elizabeth and I lived in Vancouver from 1997 to 2002, and one of our Sunday rituals came to be walking a labyrinth. The Labyrinth was a replica of the one found on the floor of the Cathedral at Chartres, France, and it was painted on the floor of the gymnasium at St. Paul's Anglican Church in Vancouver's West End. The first time I walked it was the most dramatic for me. I was in my early fifties at the time, and it gave me an insight into life.

In a sense, the labyrinth for me was like life, in that it had twists and turns, but all the while I was heading toward the centre. It didn't matter what direction I was going, as long as I was walking intentionally.

When I first stepped into the Labyrinth's path, it looked as though the centre was pretty close, but as I walked, looking down to follow the narrow pathway, I suddenly found myself on the other side of the labyrinth, wondering how I got there. This experience repeated itself as I walked slowly along, following the many turns.

Time and again I was struck by the thought that even though at times I seemed to be heading away, if I stayed on the path, and kept moving intentionally, I would end up in the centre.

There may not be a labyrinth near you, but perhaps this little story will help you remember that as you travel on your journey, if you do it with clear intention, you will end up where you want to be. Of course the journey itself is the most important part!

Purpose and Health

Years ago, Henry David Thoreau said "Most men lead lives of quiet desperation and go to the grave with the song still in them".

A sense of purpose will help you live longer

Having a sense of meaning, or purpose, not only gives you a reason to get up in the morning, but it will help you live longer. A Hungarian study published in 2005 found that of the 12,460 middle-aged men and women studied, those who felt their lives had meaning had much lower rates of cancer and heart disease than those who didn't feel that way. The *Blue Zone Project*, which studies some of the longest-lived people in the world, discovered that having a sense of purpose was common among centenarians.

Finding a sense of purpose can be difficult, so Richard Leider, author of *Something to Live For: Finding Your Way in the Second Half of Life* came up with a formula: *G+V+P=C*. In other words, make a list of what you consider to be your Gifts, Values and Passions, then identify your top quality in each category. Use these to reveal your "Calling".

People who have studied longevity and happiness say your work can really help you feel your life has purpose. Men have retired, and died a few short years later, largely because they had so much of their identity and meaning tied up in their jobs, that when they left them, it was as though they left themselves behind.

Even if your job isn't all that great, having a sense of accomplishment, and just as important, having an income, can give a sense of purpose.

A recent European study that tracked 16,827 people for 12 years found that those who retired early had a 51 percent higher mortality rate than those who kept working. And a study of 3500 Shell Oil employees published in 2005 showed that those who retired at 55 were twice as likely to die during the following ten years as people the same age who continued to work.

Your faith can keep you well

Harold G. Koenig, M.D., professor of psychiatry at Duke University says: "People who feel their life is part of a larger plan and are guided by their spiritual values have stronger immune systems, lower blood pressure, a lower risk of heart attack and cancer, and heal faster and live longer".

More than 2000 studies in recent years have analyzed the correlation between health and religious faith. These studies found, among other things, that people who attend a religious service at least four times a month are less likely to be depressed, or feel chronic stress. They are less likely to engage in risky behaviour too. A study published in the journal *Demography* in 1999 tracked 20,000 Americans and found that white people who regularly attended church lived an average of seven years longer than their secular counterparts, and black people lived fourteen years longer!

Duke University's professor Koenig says people who believe in God often feel that in itself is the reward that gives life meaning. I would argue that you don't have to be a regular churchgoer to have these benefits, but you do have to have a faith in something greater than you, and you must have regular spiritual practices, such as prayer and meditation. The advantage of going to church is that it gives you a social outing, increasing your sense of fulfillment and well-being.

My own experience with spiritual growth bears that out. I had a spiritual awakening in 1983 that profoundly changed my life. One of the benefits was that I no longer got as uptight about things as I had in the past. Prior to this I felt as if I were in a tiny boat being tossed around on a stormy ocean, and now I feel as though I am sitting calmly in the deep, where I barely register the storm waves on the surface.

So there you have it: a sense of purpose, or mission; a feeling of connection to something greater; and doing work that feels meaningful, including volunteering, can make you feel more happy and fulfilled, and keep you living longer.

Singing Out A Life

My brother, one of our sisters, two nieces, my dad and I spent Monday to Thursday on a 24-hour death watch as my mother slowly slipped away. She died Thursday afternoon at about 3:15. It was a sad, but also a rich and fulfilling time as we sat, sometimes alone, sometimes with four or five of us around the hospital bed, with mom in a coma. We reminisced about times passed, remembering good times and bad and just talked about everyday things.

Every ten minutes or so, one of us would swab mom's mouth out with a wet sponge stick provided by the hospital, as she lay there breathing steadily, but more weakly as each day passed.

I have met with a number of people who have been with parents as they died, and all have said it was a gift to be there. I now understand why they say that. It was truly a gift to me to be with my family as our mother passed away.

I had dreamt for years about singing a couple of special songs for her, always assuming it would be at her funeral, but I got the chance to "sing her home" instead. On the last day, I brought my guitar with me, and as she was taking her final breaths (a certain kind of breathing known as Cheyne-Stokes breathing). I sang *Angel Band*, *I'll Fly Away* and *Wayfaring Stranger*. Shortly after I finished the last song, she died.

If you're in midlife, you are probably thinking, like I am, that we're getting to the stage where we are soon to be "the next in the box." Losing a parent is a milestone you can expect to pass sometime during midlife, if it hasn't happened sooner. It is one that will change you. You might be left feeling like a "midlife orphan," or that you are now the head of the family, or both. Maybe we have been putting off some things that now feel more urgent.

If your parents are still alive, and there is something you want to tell them, such as how much you love and appreciate them now might be a good time! Sing them home while you can.

Namaste.

SECTION FOUR

DON'T BLOW YOUR RELATIONSHIPS

Full Throttle Relationships

Tell Her You Love Her

A few years ago I was coaching a farm couple over the phone. During previous sessions we had covered their values, life goals, financial plans, and marketing strategy for their organic dairy products. This time we were talking about communication, and how they could make their good marriage even better.

Jim truly loved Helen, and showed it by working hard. He made sure they had enough money for her to pursue personal interests such as art classes, and to take at least three weeks of family holidays every year. About the only thing he didn't do to show his love was tell her he loved her!

During the coaching session, I guided Jim to work up the courage say the words. When he eventually managed to get them out, Helen, on the other extension, began to cry.

I have met many men who struggle to compliment family members, or say words of endearment to their wives. It is almost as though they fear something horrible will happen if they say the words.

A woman, hungry for the words wrote me:

Dear Noel,

My husband has NEVER been one to let me know how he feels about me ... even after all these years. He almost never compliments me. If I do something extra special for him, I never even hear about it. He cannot express his feelings for me and I don't understand. I ask him to just let me know how he feels in his heart and he cops out and says he doesn't know how to express himself. Just because he comes home every night doesn't mean to me that he loves me. This has become a very big issue over the years because I'm very verbal about my feelings for him and enjoy letting him know how I feel about him. I know his Dad never discussed feelings with any of the family, nor did he ever hand out compliments or praise of any kind. He was a very hard man to live with.

I suggested to my husband that I make him a list of things he could say from time to time, so as to give him some sort of clue as to what I'm expecting. Is this a bad idea? I feel desperate, at times, for acknowledgement and words of love but my husband (a good man) seems to have no need of any of that and can't see why I would. I know I'm going through menopause but *is* he? Thanks for your time. Sarah

Whatever the reason, it works against men. According to Shaunti Feldhahn in her book *For Women Only: What You Need to Know about the Inner Lives of Men*,[11] women want to know (read hear) they are loved, more than anything else. Men want to know (read hear) they are respected.

You might feel you are respected if you are relied upon, asked to do special tasks, and in general treated in a respectful manor. Although you like to be told you are doing a good job, you can live without it if you are treated with respect. But you must receive some kind of recognition. I have met many men whose fathers neither said nor did anything to show their sons they respected and appreciated them, and long after their fathers are dead these sons still wish they had received some kind of praise from their dads. And guess what? They don't praise their sons either.

A woman wants to hear she is loved. She also wants to hear she is appreciated, respected, cherished, and wanted. As do we all.

So here is a suggestion: Risk telling your wife you love her, that she is desirable, she is a great wife, you appreciate her, and she still makes your heart beat a little faster. Don't worry about the consequences. Chances are you'll like them!

Ms. Feldhahn learned from the men she interviewed that the most important thing to the men was that their wives knew they loved them deeply. A good way for you to guarantee that your wife knows that is to tell her.

---

[11] Feldhahn, Shaunti; *For Women Only: What You Need to Know about the Inner Lives of Men;* Multnomah Books, a division of Random House; New York, NY; 2004.

Sorting out the Holidays

Christmas and other major holidays can be among the most trying times for divorced parents, especially those that are newly divorced, and most especially those who have a lot of conflict and bitterness.

Elizabeth and I have five children between us, and when we first got married, she had been divorced for eight years, and her former husband had died. That left her side of things flexible.

On the other hand, my ex-wife and I had only been apart for about three years, and although we got along quite civilly, it didn't take too much to stir things up. Our three kids were older too, with the youngest, Matthew, being thirteen.

Christmas brought a bit of tension.

The first year, my ex and I had agreed that Matthew would be at my place for Christmas morning, and then go to her place for dinner. I wasn't sure what to decide about my oldest two. They were eighteen and twenty-one, and living on their own, so I didn't figure it was up to us to decide where they should go. My ex figured we should. They all came to my new home, and my ex assumed all three would then go to her house.

Christmas day came, and we were all having lots of fun at my house. The next thing you know, the phone rang. It was my ex, very angry, and wondering where the kids were. I looked at the clock, and realized it was almost the time she and I had agreed they would be at her place. I felt guilty and resentful at the same time. I was having fun with the kids, and didn't want them to leave. Besides, there were still a few minutes left before they had to be at her place, so what was she doing calling me already? Shouldn't she at least wait till they were late? Just the same, I had agreed, so I had to tell them it was time to go to their mother's house.

We got through that without a major battle, and without the kids having to feel bad, but we knew we had to be very clear, and respectful of each other's wishes in the future, knowing we each would rather have the kids with us through the whole day.

One thing we both had as a true priority was to make sure we did not put the kids in a tug-of-war between us, which would put them in an impossible situation, and is simply not fair.

Here are a few simple concepts that worked for us and may work for you:

- Never send messages to each other through the kids, as in "Tell your mother ... blah blah blah". Invariably you'll slip a negative tone into the message, and the kids, who love you both, end up offending, or defending one or the other parent. "What the blankety blank does he mean by that?" "You tell him I'll see him in blankety blank before I agree to that!"

- Always plan holiday times with the kids well in advance, especially if they are still living at home. A month is good. A year is better. And do it in writing. That way no one says, "I thought you agreed so-and-so would happen." And the other says, "No, you said such-and-such", and the war is on.

- Be flexible. A reasonable strategy is to ask the other what they want, and then fit your schedule around it, if at all possible. If they say they don't know what they will be doing, then you tell them what you want. They will either agree, or say they want to do something at that same time, in which case, if it works for you, you can say okay to that, and then set your own time.

Why not have festivus?

Our kids are all adults now, and they have in-laws to consider as well, plus we have our parents to work into the situation, so this year we are having a family get-together on December 11. That way we won't interfere with anyone else's Christmas plans, and whoever can make it to our place for Christmas dinner is welcome. If they can't, that's fine too.

As more couples split and more families are blended, many are choosing to come together for Christmas before or after the 25th. Consider this; you can get together the long weekend in August because it suits everyone. You still have the tree (could be a poplar in the backyard), the lights (your patio lights), the food that means Christmas (deep fried turkey anyone?), but a lot less of the pressures.

I heard of a woman who gathers her family on a different day and calls it Festivus – the holiday created by George's parents on Seinfeld. It's a holiday to put the *FUN* back in "dysfunctional".

Three Magic Words

You're a man with a problem. You tell your buddies. They immediately offer a variety of solutions. This does not offend you. It makes sense, right?

It doesn't make sense to women! Women, in general, tend to solve problems out loud. A woman struggling with a problem will get together with a friend and talk to her about it. She will describe the situation, tell how she feels about it, wonder out loud what to do about it, come up with some possible solutions, and eventually decide what she needs to do. Her friend mostly just listens, and maybe asks a few questions to help her explore it more fully. She may offer a solution, but that won't be the first thing she does.

Now, put a man and a woman together (say you and your wife). She is struggling with a problem. She tells you the problem, and your immediate response is to ask her if she has tried so-and-so solution. She says no, she doesn't want to do that.

What about solution X, you ask? Nope. Solution Y? Nope. Now you are getting frustrated, and she is getting mad. Pretty soon she is complaining that you aren't listening, and you have no idea what she is talking about. You have offered plenty of solutions, and *she* hasn't listened to any of them!

If you have ever been in this situation, and especially if you are likely to be in it again, here are three magic words you can use: **"Tell Me More."**

That's it. It's that simple. When your wife (or daughter, or girlfriend, or any female) complains to you about a problem she is facing, instead of telling her what she needs to do, just say, 'Tell me more". When she gets over the shock, she *will* tell you more.

Maybe she comes home from work and says, "I don't know what I am going to do about Tom. He just isn't carrying his weight on this project." You say, "Tell me more." As the conversation carries on, you can add questions that will help her process the problem, such as "How did that work?" or "Where will you go from here?" or "What would you LIKE to have happen?" You get the idea. Notice I am using all the "W" words (where, when, why, what) that require the person to answer with more than a "yes" or "no."

She will talk about all angles of the problem for a while. You just keep listening (and I mean you should actually LISTEN, not just act as though you are). Eventually she may even ask you if you have a suggestion, at which time it is okay to give it.

BUT DON"T BE ATTACHED TO HER TAKING IT!

Next time your wife is struggling with something, *try it,* and see whether she doesn't appreciate you for it.

Power up your three words ... "Tell me more."

The Dangerous Four

If your wife complains that you don't listen, or that you are "mean," you might want to take a look at your communication style when you and your true love have a disagreement.

Dr. John Gottman and his wife, Julie, established the Gottman Institute in Seattle, Washington. Gottman has studied relationships, especially marriage relationships, for years, and is unique as far as I know in that years ago he began "wiring couples up" when they were having an argument. He would video them, and have various other monitors to get feedback on their physical reactions to the stress of having a marital tiff.

Gottman has learned a great deal about marriage relationships, and says he can predict with more than 90% accuracy whether a couple's marriage will last after interviewing them for 20 minutes or so. He says in general, if there are at least five positive statements for each negative one in a marriage (or any other relationship for that matter), the relationship will be healthy. But he has discovered there are four types of exchanges, which no marriage can survive over the long-term.

These are:

- criticism
- defensiveness
- contempt
- stonewalling

The first two may sound a lot like anger and disagreement but there is a big difference. For example, John might say to Valerie, "It makes me mad that you didn't give me that message from my boss. He was irritated that I wasn't at the meeting and I hate looking irresponsible." OR he could say, "When are you ever going to learn to be responsible! As usual, you screwed up and didn't give me that message from my boss. What do you use for brains?"

The first exchange will not hurt your marriage provided there is an ongoing balance of five positive interactions to one negative; but the nature of the second exchange is too hostile for any marriage to survive for long. The anger is not the issue. It is the insult and derision that is destructive.

Stonewalling is common when a couple has had an upsetting fight and one of the partners either physically or emotionally leaves the room. This is "crazy-making" for the partner who is left behind and wants to get things resolved.

Dr. Gottman's research shows that 85% of the time men do the stonewalling. The Love Lab has discovered a difference in our sex that explains why. In a heated argument, men become more intensely upset physiologically than women. A man continues to be distressed long after a woman has calmed down.

During the argument, and even after it is settled, you are often still flooded with adrenalin, and so wound up you can barely contain yourself. As you can't switch your system off, you are tempted to simply withdraw.

If this happens only occasionally, it is probably not a big deal, especially if you come back later and finishes the discussion. But if stonewalling is your standard approach to marital conflict, the chances of your marriage surviving are pretty slim, according to Gottman.

Escalating to Abuse

There are many abusive relationships, and the ones we usually hear about are where men are physically violent with women. There are other forms of abuse though, and I have experienced some emotional abuse myself, in a former marriage. When any of the four exchanges escalate or become chronic they become abuse, ranging from verbal abuse to mental cruelty.

In a letter to me, Robert M. tells of his struggle with an emotionally abusive wife. He writes:

> I am 45 and after 23 years of marriage I left my wife. She was never really a partner in our relationship because she was always living on the edge. She struggled with depression, anger, suicide and panic. I told her she only went over the edge 10% of the time but she was on the edge 100% of the time. Thus we (my children and I) lived walking on eggshells for many years. The kids are grown and I don't have to be the calming force in the house anymore. I don't have to be in the house at all and that is what I have chosen.

Robert goes on to explain he realized his situation after reading about domestic violence aimed at women. He was already following most of their suggestions for avoiding violence. Perhaps you find yourself in this place too, or need to pick up a pamphlet and see if things sound familiar to you.

Possibly, like Robert, you have a "code phrase" you use with your children when things begin to escalate. You may, like him, remove yourself and children from the home to somewhere you actually feel safe.

One of the things that worked against Robert was that he never told anyone. Are you keeping your situation a secret? Are you avoiding sharing this because it would force you to deal with it and you just don't know how? Robert says, "I came from a family where there was no fighting or yelling. No one was ever mad at me. I didn't know what to do with this person that was so angry and depressed."

Robert also pointed out that many men retire before their younger wives, and look forward to enjoying their freedom from work. Then they find that their wife resents that they are out having fun, while she is tied down nine to five and two tired to play afterwards. If you have "too much fun" do you "pay dearly?" If you are, like many men "afraid to have friends, go out with friends, have interests outside of their wife, go to bed when they want to, watch TV if they want to, etc.," maybe you need to take Robert's advice, "Get rid of your wife and have all the fun you want."

Living for years with someone who treats you with contempt, criticizes your every move, puts you constantly on the defensive, until you're just so emotional you have to walk away, or as in Robert's case, run and hide is living in an abusive relationship. It can turn you off women in general, which is a real shame because there are a lot of good ones out there.

Robert walked away from his abusive relationship, knowing he needed to in order to feel "good enough" in his own eyes. Violence of any kind, particularly when children are involved, must be addressed not avoided. Seek help, get yourself some support, and be sure to share so your secret loses its power.

Shift Gears in Midlife

Gentling the Beast

Many men (and probably women too), by the time they get to midlife, seem to feel they are in a dead-end marriage, or that they are missing something in their marriage, or perhaps missing something in their life, that they think they could find if they weren't married, or were married to someone else. No doubt that is sometimes true.

But it may be equally true that over the years as a couple you have lost touch with what you liked about each other originally, and have begun to treat each other badly. Resentment and bitterness may have grown to the point where you don't want to be together any more. The most distressing part is if you become verbally abusive as well, saying nasty things to your partner.

Be Kind

I am dismayed by how many men become mean to their wives/partners when they are depressed and irritable (which are common symptoms of midlife transitions). I know when you are feeling irritable it is easy to lose patience with almost any-one, and that is pretty much unavoidable as far as I can tell. What is avoidable is to become mean and nasty. There is no excuse for that. You may need to let people know you just can't talk right now, but to use cruel words is not acceptable.

The late Mike Steinhauer, a Cree elder who was my mentor for many years taught the four principles of a balanced life:

- Love (expressed as kindness)
- Sharing (your time, talents, possessions, etc.)

- Truth (as in speaking and living your truth)
- Strength (perseverance, or determination)

Of these four, treating others with kindness and respect will go the furthest toward harmonious relationships, and will help you make it through your midlife transition with dignity.

So many emails and phone calls I get from women talk about how their husbands have turned mean with not only them, but with their children as well. Relationships are often damaged for years because of careless and unkind words. One woman wrote to say she desperately wanted help trying to figure out how to deal with her husband of 24 years. He was forty-five, and during the past year had become withdrawn, defensive, uncommunicative and sometimes downright mean with the words he uses. He recently left home. She is at her wit's end.

I suggested she figure out what she needs in her life, as well as what behaviour she will not put up with from him (e.g., verbal or any other kind of abuse). She has, of course, been trying to get him to talk to her about what's going on with him, but the more she pushes, the more reticent and defensive he gets. As that approach does not work, I suggested she let him be. I also assured her that he would get through this transition, after which he may or may not come back to her. In either case, she needs to figure out what is important in her life.

We are men. Our responsibility is to protect and care for our families, our communities, and our part of the world. Yes midlife transitions are hard, disorienting, frightening, and confusing, but while we go through them there is no excuse for abusing those that love us.

If you have forgotten what brought you together in the first place, you have lost what Dr. John Gottman, calls your "Fondness and Admiration System". He states:

> Fondness and admiration are two of the most crucial elements in a rewarding and long-lasting romance. Although happily married couples may feel driven to distraction at times by their partner's personality flaws, they still feel that the person they married is worthy of honour and respect. When this sense is completely missing from a marriage, the relationship cannot be revived.[12]

Be Fair

Many women tell me that they don't know what is going on with their men. Here is a fairly typical example:

> Hello Noel, I have been married for 10 years. My husband is 44. We both work. My husband was always so sweet and kind to me, but about 6 months ago I saw a change in him. He always called me when he was away, always told me he loved me, missed me. Now if I say I miss you or love you he turns off the conversation, also he NEVER calls when he gone now. I try not to say I love you or miss you, or call him. I feel so lost I don't know what to do. I feel like he has died. Please can you give me any advice? I've started seeing a counsellor (he won't). He is just so mad all the time when he comes home he's mad, he blames me for everything that happens at home and at work. Help.

---

[12] Gottman, Dr. John; *The Seven Principles For Making Marriage Work*; Three Rivers Press; New York, NY; 1999.

Often women write to say their husbands have left home after ten, or fifteen, or twenty-five years of marriage, saying they suddenly realized they never did love their wives, and want to be free. The women are devastated.

I have no judgement about separation and divorce. I was divorced from my second wife during my forties. It was her idea, but it was a relief to both of us. What seems unfair to me is that many men treat their wives disrespectfully. Some become downright mean, and say things they never would have said when they were "normal." That is not fair to their wives.

When you are feeling irritable for some reason it seems easiest to say nasty things to people who love you. But I don't think that makes it okay. I have even heard men say they can't help themselves; when they get angry, they just blurt things out. But I have noticed these guys manage to control what they say to men bigger than they are!

The other thing almost every woman who emails me complains about is that their men won't talk to them about what they are feeling. I know having your wife badger you about what you are feeling can be irritating, as half the time you don't know yourself. But again, it isn't necessary to be mean when responding to her request that you talk about what you are feeling.

Here are a few strategies that can help you have honest conversations with your wife, even if only to let her know you are feeling irritable and don't want to talk right now:

- Use "I" statements. When we are having emotional conversations, at home or work, it is very easy to slip into "you" statements, which tend to point the finger and blame others for whatever is going wrong. All this does is make the others feel angry and defensive. "I" statements allow the others to hear what you are saying without having to become defensive. It makes communication much easier.

- Remind yourself that even if you are feeling irritable, the people around you deserve to be treated respectfully. This is particularly true for your family. Even if you and your wife are separating, acquit yourself with dignity. You will be glad you did.
- If you are going to have a potentially emotional conversation, pick a time when you are rested, not hungry, not pressed for time, and are not likely to have any interruptions.

Midlife can be tumultuous, and I know a number of couples who have separated for a period of time, then got back together, sometimes months and sometimes a year or two later, and found their new relationship very satisfying. If you make it a habit to be kind to each other, you will limit the emotional damage, so that if you do split for a while, you can still get back together.

Mike Steinhauer described love as being demonstrated by kindness and compassion. Love is not a feeling but rather an action. And if we treat our partners kindly, even if we do not feel "in love" with them at the moment, it may save a lot of pain in the long run.

Seeing the Flaws

At midlife you are often dissatisfied with many aspects of life, including your marriage. Perhaps you are remembering the glory days when you were younger and your partner was more the way she was when you first got married. The way you thought she was going to stay! You may think you married the wrong partner, and fantasize about being with a different partner, especially a younger one.

The Jennifer Syndrome

I don't know whether you saw the 1970 movie Love Story. I didn't. I figured any movie with the insipid tagline "Love means never having to say you're sorry" was too dopey to bother with. However, one of the main characters, Jennifer Cavalleri, has become the epitome of the pure, high-spirited young woman with plenty of panache. She is the kind that men might fantasize about, especially men in midlife crises. Some even go out and look for a 'Jennifer', when they are trying desperately to hide the fact that their own youthfulness is fading. Psychologists and doctors refer to it as "Jennifer Syndrome."

That is what my friend, Keith, did when he was 55. He had an affair with an attractive woman in her thirties. He left his wife, moved in with his lover, and lived in a state of aroused confusion for three years. He felt guilty about leaving his wife, but was attracted to the younger woman like a moth to a flame.

"When I am with her, I feel younger, more alive," he told me. Eventually he left the younger woman, and went back to his wife, who agreed to try to work through the pain and sense of betrayal to forge a new relationship. As far as I know they are still married.

As the old saying goes, men marry women expecting them to stay the same, and they don't. And women marry men expecting them to change, and they don't.

At any rate, many men and women are dissatisfied with their marriage at midlife. In general, if they hang in there, it passes, and they go on to a very satisfying older age, if they are both willing to adapt to the personal changes each is going through.

A while ago I ran across this little story in *Who Ordered This Truckload of Dung? Inspiring stories for welcoming life's difficulties* by Ajahn Brahm, and thought I would pass it on:

GRATITUDE

After a wedding ceremony in Singapore a few years ago, the father of the bride took his new son-in-law aside to give him some advice on how to keep the marriage long and happy. "You probably love my daughter a lot," he said to the young man. "Oh yes!" the young man sighed. "And you probably think that she is the most wonderful person in the world," the old man continued.

"She's sooooo perfect in each and every way," the young man cooed.

"That's how it is when you get married," said the old man. "But after a few years, you will begin to see the flaws in my daughter. When you do begin to notice her faults, I want you to remember this. If she didn't have those faults to begin with, Son-in-law, she would have married someone much better than you!"

A reminder, then, be grateful for the flaws you find in your partner because if s/he didn't have those faults from the start, s/he would have been able to marry someone much better than you.

Marital Discord

At midlife, marriages often go through some rocky times. I believe it is partly because men and women are both going through their "midlife trials" (menopause for her and andropause for him), and that, along with poor communication skills for many men, can lead to problems.

Marital discord is destructive to your health

More and more research in the new field of psychoneuroimmunology is showing that stress of all kinds is hard on our health. For example, a study done a few years ago of 79 married couples, showed that colds and upper respiratory infections could be predicted fairly reliably to follow a marital fight or other hassles within 3-4 days.

Now, there is going to be some discord at times in any marriage or close relationship, but the better you are at handling these hassles, the less stress, and literally the healthier you will be.

In general, the better you know your partner, the lower the number of fights. So the question is, how well do you know your partner?

Understanding can provide considerable relief. For example, if your wife has a pattern of venting every so often, you will recognize that it is not specific to you, you just happen to be in the room. Understanding this you can choose to remove yourself till it's over, or remain without taking it personally or getting on the defensive. OR You may know that you are in a foul mood every year-end of your business and not good company. You could share this with your spouse and arrange for some alone time.

Dr. John Gottman founded what the media termed "The Love Lab", where he conducted much of his research on couples' interactions. He made some interesting findings, including identifying three basic types of marriages.

- **Stormy marriages**, where there are big explosive fights followed by intense and passionate periods of making-up.
- **Normal or "Ideal" marriages** as described by marriage counsellors, where the couple has periodic fights or arguments, but has good communication skills and can resolve conflicts.
- **Quiet marriages**, where the couple "never fights" (psychologists have always assumed these kinds of marriages must be unsatisfying with a lot of dissatisfaction seething beneath the surface, but Gottman's research shows that is not necessarily so).

So fighting like storm troopers is no more harmful to your relationship than floating quietly through your marriage. All three types can be very happy and long-lasting if you learn to cope well with the stressors within your relationship. Good communication eliminates a lot of stress, as does understanding your partner. So... if you start paying attention to the details and setting your own boundaries you will provide yourself with the tools for a healthier you and a healthier marriage.

Sometimes you may think you married the wrong person, and sometimes that is true. But sometimes YOU aren't such a great partner yourself!

Facing Divorce

I first heard from Rick when he called after hearing me on a Canadian Broadcasting Corporation radio show where I was talking about midlife challenges. Rick's wife had left a few months earlier, but it was kind of dragged out. She had gone to a different city for a couple of years to get a college diploma, and then worked in Central America for a while. Rick kept the home fires burning, waiting for her to come back, until she told him on the phone a few months ago that she wasn't coming back!

Of course this put Rick into a tail spin. He felt betrayed, lonely, hurt, angry... all the feelings you would expect under the circumstances. He wrestled with an important question. I'll let him explain:

> When I was going through my depression and the terribly cold weather in January, and glommed onto the idea of going to Vancouver Island, after the separation and selling the house, and getting a temporary job till it was all settled, I always had in the back of my mind the question. "Was I making the right decision(s)?" especially when I was so low. I never thought my depression, lack of energy, anxiety and doom and gloom attitude would lessen, if not go away. I also worried that I was not "getting over it" fast enough ... In making the plans, was I fooling myself, or was I correct in doing SOMETHING to get me over it, and give me hope, and something to look forward to?

Rick said the book *Life After Divorce* by Sharon Wegscheider-Cruse, recommended by his therapist, saved him.

I have learned, through my own experiences with widowhood and divorce, and from talking to many others who have gone through major upheavals, that it is very tempting to make big changes in your life when you are facing big transitions. Transitions have three stages:

- **An Ending**
- **A Neutral Zone**
- **A Beginning**

William Bridges in his books on transition explains the anatomy of transitions particularly well.

The **Ending Phase** can be confusing. All we know is our life felt settled and good, and then something happened and we now feel lost and confused. We are "wandering in the underworld" and we don't know why and can't seem to do anything about it.

What follows is often a feeling of "disintegration," where nothing seems to make sense. We sometimes feel as though we are failing, or malfunctioning, but it's really just the Neutral Place, where the true new beginning is gestating.

This **Neutral Time** can be very trying. By its nature, it is an unknown. It has been described as a "night sea journey". We know we have left something behind, but we do not know what or WHEN something new will replace it. My wife and I like to keep a quote by Andre Gide in mind as encouragement in the neutral time:

*"One does not discover new lands without consenting
to lose sight of the shore for a very long time."*

While you are in the neutral time, you may discover, or be offered many new choices and directions, and although tempting, some of these choices could be blind alleys.

Sometimes you have uncompleted endings from the past that hinder the completion of the transition you are in. Therapy can be very useful to help sort out which choices might lead to a fuller life and which might drag you down. For example, you might leave a negative or destructive situation or relationship, and without therapy, you are in danger of getting into a similar one without realizing it until it is too late.

New Beginnings cause problems for almost everyone. You think you should be in charge of your life, and you plan carefully to start something new. But life is not like that. Unexpected challenges invariably confront you, no matter how carefully you plan.

When you are feeling lost and stuck in some unknown swamp, it is immeasurably helpful to have someone who recognizes what is happening help you stay the course so that you don't lose heart; someone to tell you "this too shall pass." That help can come from a coach, a therapist, a support group, or a trusted friend.

Financial experts and many counsellors will tell you that the worst time to make big changes is when you are in the midst of major emotional crisis. This is particularly true of major financial decisions, such as selling a house. When you finally complete the transition, you may regret the decision. You might also be so vulnerable at the time you are selling that your judgment is impaired and you sell impulsively for significantly less than you could have obtained. I have a friend who bought a farm at about half its market value because the couple that owned it was separating, and they just wanted out!

That being said, big emotional upheavals can be the ideal time to make changes. After all, when your life is "normal" you don't think of changing, even if what you are doing is not what your soul wants you to do. Most crises are wake-up calls from your Soul, telling you to pay attention to what you are doing with your life.

In an article entitled *A House Divided* in an issue of AARP (American Association of Retired Persons) magazine says divorce among the over-50 group is on the rise, and increasingly, it is women who do the walking. AARP Magazine commissioned a survey of 1147 men and women, ages 40 to 79 that experienced a divorce in their 40s, 50s or 60s.

Here are some of the results:

- 66 percent of women reported they had asked for the divorce, compared with 41 percent of men.
- More men (26%) than women (14%) were caught off-guard by their divorce (i.e. didn't know it was coming).
- It takes longer for people over 40 to decide on divorce. About 1/3 of the women, and 21% of the men started thinking about splitting two years or longer before the actual event.
- 58% of men, compared with 37% of women, stayed in an unsatisfying marriage because of the kids. The men were more worried (justifiably) than the women about losing the kids.
- Almost half (47%) of the people surveyed had been divorced once before, when they were younger.
- 75% of women and 81% of men enjoyed a serious, exclusive relationship after their divorce – often within two years. The number one reason both gave for getting "back into action" was to prove to themselves that they were getting on with their lives. For men, sex ranked a close second.
- One in four men in their 50s, and a third in their 60s and older, said they had sex with a new partner as a means of coping with the stress of the divorce. Alcohol was the

second most frequent coping mechanism. Women used exercise and retreating into work to help them cope.

- Against society's expectations, and in spite of the pain, midlife divorce tends to leave a normal, healthy and optimistic man or woman in its wake. They reported roughly the same measures of happiness as other single Americans their own age, and those who remarried also scored very high. This was true regardless of who made the decisions to split, or how long the marriage had lasted.

You may be the instigator or the unsuspecting spouse or be dealing with a crisis outside divorce. Whatever the case, if you are moved to make sweeping changes to your life in the midst of a big transition, don't make the decisions all by yourself. As Rick says, doing SOMETHING seemed like the right thing to get him through the depression and give him hope. But he realized he needed help, so he joined a divorce support group, and talked to a therapist that he saw for three years. He also attended a retreat for recently divorced people, which he says was "gut-and-heart-wrenching and emotionally draining, but excellent."

Rick talked to friends about his plans as well, which helped. He still questioned whether he was doing the right thing in planning to sell his house and move to the coast, but at least he didn't make the decisions in a vacuum. Are they the right decisions? Time will tell. But the worst that will happen is he will wish later that he hadn't, and he can learn to live with that.

Anyone facing separation or divorce faces two big dangers:

1. Getting into another permanent relationship too soon. My own experience and what I hear from marriage and grief counsellors is that it takes about three years to recover emotionally from being widowed or divorced. It is

fine to have relationships during that time, but don't make them permanent. Chances are a person you are attracted to when you are in an emotional crisis (the Ending and the Neutral phases) is not the same type of person you will find attractive after you have established your new life, and know "who you are now."

2. Making an expensive financial mistake. At midlife you don't have much time left to recover. Get some financial advice from someone you trust (who understands financial stuff) before you make big decisions. This is especially true for investments, say, deciding what to do with the money you got from selling the house.

And remember... whenever you are in a transition – it's a transition and it will end!

Ride the Road Less Traveled

Proving You're a Man

We have no marker in our society that clearly identifies us, or defines us, as men. Initiation rituals do this in traditional societies, where the men come and take pubescent boys away from their mothers, put them through some rigorous ceremonies, teach them the roles and responsibilities of men, and bring them back to the village. From then on, the initiates are regarded as men.

We are not so lucky, and it often takes a long time for us to feel as though we are men. Barring initiation, what we really need is for our fathers to tell us they see us as men. But this seldom happens. Our fathers did not receive that kind of recognition or blessing from their fathers, nor did our grandfathers receive it from their fathers, so they did/do not know how to go about it, or that it is even necessary.

I was in my 40s before I clearly felt that I was a man, particularly around my dad. The precipitating event was small, but significant to me. Essentially, I had a disagreement with my dad about spreading fertilizer on his farm, and told him I was going to do it my way. We didn't have a big row about it, but there was something about coming up against him and not acquiescing that made a mental *click* in my mind and helped me decide I was a man.

It seems strange to me that I would be in my 40s before "feeling like a man," especially considering I was managing men in my twenties, and had held a number of responsible positions over the years. But I think that is the power of our relationships with our fathers.

As I mentioned before, the movie *8 Seconds* is a poignant example of a man trying to gain his father's love and approval. The 'boy' is the best bull rider in the world, but he never does get the one thing he longs for - his father's recognition and blessing.

Often men keep trying to prove themselves to their dads, even after their fathers are dead. Some years ago I met a fellow who had three warehouses full of classic cars, including several Rolls Royces and a couple of Duesenbergs. As we talked, it became clear he was collecting the cars in order to feel important and to prove to his dad that he was a success (read: a man).

I am sure he was not consciously aware he was doing this, but his language made it clear to me.

If you have a son it is your duty to give him your blessing, and encourage him as he goes out into the world, and let him know you see him as a man. A son who does not receive this blessing can suffer for years, dealing with feelings of low self-esteem, lack of confidence, and/or grandiosity as he strives to show you he is a man. He may become a workaholic in an effort to prove to you that he has succeeded. And while focused on the struggle to prove something to you, he fails in other things that really count, such as recognizing his own worth and being there for his family. It can also hold him back from achieving as much as he could.

Some "hero's journey folktales" tell of the young hero sleeping on the grave of his father and/or grandfather, to indicate that our job as sons is to surpass the father's accomplishments, which is how societal progress is made. Our fathers have taken us as far as they can, and now it is our turn. Many men are afraid to out-do their fathers, for fear their fathers might be angry, or hurt, or disown them. And some fathers might, but not a father who has a sense of self.

Perhaps you are lucky and your dad explicitly recognized you as a man, and maybe even had a ceremony of some kind for you. I made a special point of formally telling my sons, when they left home, that I saw them as men now, and would relate to them that way. I try hard to do so.

I mentioned that we don't have anything like an initiation ceremony in our society, but that is not quite true. **The Mankind Project** (www.mankindproject.org) has a very powerful weekend program called the *New Warrior Training Adventure* that is designed to act as an initiation for men in industrialized nations. I took the training in 1999 when I was 54 years old, and highly recommend it to any man of any age who is serious about clarifying his life mission, and being seen by his peers, and especially himself, as a man.

Have You Told Your Dad You Love Him?

I have met many men over the years that have never told their dads they love them, and whose dads have never told them, and now their dads are dead. These men live with the regret of never having spoken these words to their fathers, or heard them spoken. I did not want to be a man living with that kind of regret, yet for years I wanted to tell my dad I love him, but was afraid to. I told myself that because he was not very comfortable talking about feelings, I would make him uncomfortable by expressing mine. Thinking about it later, I realized it was actually me that would be uncomfortable, whether my dad was or not. About fifteen years ago I was at a leadership training workshop, and one of the exercises we were assigned was to name the important people in our lives, and list any we had unfinished business with. I realized It was time to tell my dad I love him.

I decided to take the easy way. Knowing I would be visiting my dad the following week, I wrote him a letter, telling him I love him. I also told him about a couple of things he had done that had hurt me, which I wished later I wouldn't have put in the letter because it muddied the water a bit.

The following week, he and I were driving together to a seminar on grazing management, and I asked him if he got my letter:

"Yup."

"Do you have anything to say about it?"

"I don't know why a person would write a letter like that."

"I just wanted you to know you are important to me."

"Well, you kids are important to me to."

And that was the end of the conversation. But I noticed that our relationship changed in subtle ways after that. There was a bit more openness between us. My dad is still alive and doing well at age 95, but when he does die, which will likely be sometime during the next ten years, I will not have to live with the regret of never having told him I love him.

How about you? Are you one of the lucky ones, whose dad freely tells you he loves you and is proud of you? And to whom you respond to in kind? (I try to be such a father to my children.) If not, and your dad is still alive, when will you tell him you love him?

If you find the courage to tell your father you love him, then why not take it one step further and thank him for some of the things he's done to make your life better. Or use your thank you's to open the door so you can say, "Dad, I love you." The list below was published on **www.menstuff.org**

Have you thanked your Dad for:
- A childhood experience when your father came through for you. (e.g., when he missed work to come to the big game; when he put in extra hours to pay for something you really wanted; when the neighbour's dog scared you, and suddenly your father was beside you).
- A life lesson your father taught you, by words or example. (e.g., The time he modeled generosity for you by giving to someone who was down and out; when he taught you fiscal responsibility by not charging something he wanted but couldn't afford; when he controlled his anger toward someone who insulted him; the respectful, caring way he treated his own elderly parents.)

- Financial support and material presents. Grown children often criticize their fathers for having spent too much time working and not enough time with them. Even if you're right that his priorities were wrong, even if you raise your own children very differently, reflect on this: You enjoyed summer camp, you spent a lot of time during your teenage years talking on the phone, it was important to you to dress stylishly and your father paid for all that!

Time presses on and moments are quickly lost. You may hesitate a second and the chance to say I love you slips away for another decade. Don't lose it out of fear, embarrassment or bitterness. Expressing your gift of love can lift others emotionally and make you feel like a better person.

IT'S RUNNING ROUGH

Engine Maintenance a Must

Cell Phones and Your Brain

I wrote an article a few years ago about a British military study that showed cell phones interfere with brain waves. Here is another study, this time from Dr. Daniel Amen's newsletter.

To Your Brain Health, Daniel G. Amen, MD, his website: http://www.amenclinic.com/

Talking on a cell phone excites the brain, Italian researchers find - but they don't yet know whether that's good or bad.

Could this affect your brain? Yes, according to neurologist Paolo Maria Rossini, MD, PhD, research director at Fatebenefratelli Hospital in Rome and his colleagues. The researchers say they have "shown definitively" that talking on a cell phone increases electrical activity on the side of the head where the cell phone is held. The effect mostly wears off within an hour.

Rossini's team studied 15 healthy young men for the impact of cell phone use. They found that electrical activity was enhanced in the side of the brain the cell phone is on, but not on the other side. "It could be argued that long-lasting and repeated exposure to electromagnetic fields, linked with intense use of cellular phones in daily life, might be harmful or beneficial in brain-diseased subjects," Rossini and colleagues concluded. "Further studies are needed."

So, are you safe when using your cell phone? The World Health Organization (WHO) says there have been reports of cell phones affecting brain activity, but they concluded these effects "are small and have no apparent health significance." The FDA says, "Available scientific evidence does not show that any health problems are associated with using wireless phones," but it also notes," there is no proof that wireless phones are absolutely safe." The American Cancer Society says it's "unlikely" that phones cause cancer.

Dr. Mercola's website has a lot of information about cell phones and health, and he says they are a health hazard. However, if you have no choice but to use a cell phone, you will find a list of the most and least dangerous at this website:

http://gizmodo.com/5355480/a-guide-to-cell-phone-radiation-so-you-dont-fry-your-brains

I read a statistic some months back saying the accident rate for people talking on cell phones while driving is the same as for drunk driving. Now that's a proven statistic! Are you safe?

Be Proactive: Limit the amount of time you talk on your cell phone. Switch it to the other side on a 50/50 split. Don't talk on your cell phone while you are driving.

Driving and Sunburn

Dermatologists are reporting an increase in precancerous skin spots and skin damage on the left side of drivers' faces and arms, according to an article in *Bottom Line Health* (http://www.bottomlinesecrets.com/article.html?article_id=42122) newsletter. The reason: the sun's damaging ultra-violet A (UVA) rays pass right through a car window - even if it's tinted. (UVB rays are blocked by window glass.) Even driving for only 15 minutes can cause damage to your skin.

Many men eschew sunscreen because they feel it is "girly" or because they say it feels too greasy and uncomfortable when it mixes with their sweat. However, the industry has come far over the last years, led by a big push from athletes who want protection without the sting of melting sunscreen burning their eyes, or making their grip slippery. Now there are many high quality sunscreens on the market that leave you grease free. An added benefit is that they moisturize your skin and who doesn't need that!

Men who are shaving their heads, as is a popular look today, or who refuse to wear hats and are beginning to thin on top, also need to use sunscreen on their pates. Just visit a home for our elderly and look at all the men who have patches of cancer flaking away on the tops of their heads, and you may reconsider if rubbing on some sunscreen isn't worth doing now.

Be Proactive: Before you get in your vehicle, apply sunscreen that's labelled 'broad spectrum' and/or 'UVA/UVB block' with a sun-protection factor (SPF) of at least 15.

Fibre and a Healthy Heart

Increasing dietary fibre intake to at least 25 grams per day from varied sources gives significant protection against cardiovascular disease. Researchers presumed that fibre intakes of 30- 35 grams per day would likely provide an even greater protective effect.

The results of a study published in the *American Journal of Clinical Nutrition* add to a growing body of evidence linking higher dietary fibre intake with a lower risk of heart disease. Nearly 6,000 men and women were selected from participants in an eight-year trial designed to evaluate the effect of antioxidants on cancer and heart disease.

The highest insoluble dietary fibre intakes were associated with reduced risks of obesity and elevated waist-to-hip ratio, blood pressure, cholesterol, triglycerides, and homocysteine.

Fibre from cereals was associated with a lower body mass index, blood pressure, and homocysteine concentration; fibre from vegetables with a lower blood pressure and homocysteine concentration; and fibre from fruit with a lower waist-to-hip ratio and blood pressure. Fibre from dried fruit or nuts and seeds was associated with a lower body mass index, waist-to-hip ratio, and glucose concentrations.

The results indicate that 25 grams dietary fibre per day is the minimum required to protect against cardiovascular disease, and that total dietary fibre intakes of 30-35 grams per day will likely provide an even greater protective effect.

Be Proactive: Increase your intake of dietary fibre to between 25 and 25 grams per day. Add high fibre cereal along with dried fruits and nuts to your diet if you're not already eating them.

> Excerpted from American Journal of Clinical Nutrition, Vol. 82, No. 6, 1185-1194, December 2005

Calcium and Colorectal Cancer

Men who get the most calcium have lower risks of colorectal cancer. A new study published in the *American Journal of Clinical Nutrition* analyzed over 45,000 Swedish men with no history of cancer who were between the ages of 45 and 79. Their food intake and diet were analyzed and they were followed for an average of 6.7 years.

Men whose calcium intake was in the top one-fourth of participants had a 32 percent lower risk of developing colorectal cancer than those in the bottom fourth. Dairy, the main source of calcium in Swedish diets, had the greatest protective effect on the colon. Men who consumed seven or more servings of dairy per day reduced the risk to 54 percent below that of men whose intake was less than two servings per day.

In an editorial in the same issue, researchers added that in addition to calcium, vitamin D might have also played a major role in the reduction of colorectal cancer seen in these men.

Be Proactive: Talk to your doctor about your calcium and vitamin D intake, and the best ways to introduce these into your health program. Start now so you lower your risk for colorectal cancer later in life.

American Journal of Clinical Nutrition, Vol. 83, No. 3, 667-673, March 2006.

Diet Changes and Prostate

In his book, *Reducing Your Risk: The Power of Your Plate,* Dr. Andrew Weil estimated that 75 percent of all prostate cancers could be prevented by lifestyle changes. I believe dietary measures are particularly important as protective strategies. For instance, diets high in saturated fat have been linked to a higher risk of prostate cancer, offering one more reason for men to limit their intake of red meat and full-fat dairy products. But regular consumption of the following foods can lower your risk.

Fruits and vegetables: Men who regularly eat tomatoes, tomato products, or cruciferous vegetables (such as broccoli, kale, and cabbage) are less likely to develop prostate cancer. The carotenoid lycopene is believed to be the protective compound in tomatoes; other food sources of lycopene include watermelon and pink grapefruit. Crucifers are rich in phytochemicals that may protect against cancer. And produce in general is a good source of fibre, which may reduce prostate cancer risk by helping to eliminate excess hormones from the body.

Soy foods: Whole soy foods such as tofu, soy milk, and tempeh contain isoflavones, plant estrogens that appear to help protect against both prostate cancer and breast cancer. Soy supplements may not offer the same benefits as soy foods. The only caution here is to make sure these products are labelled "Non-GMO". They can be harder to find, but there is increasing evidence that GMO (genetically modified) foods are not safe.

Fish: Men who eat fish a few times a week have a lower risk of prostate cancer. The omega-3 fatty acids in fish (such as salmon and sardines) may suppress the growth of tumour cells.

Ground flax seeds: Flax meal is rich in omega-3s as well as lignans, phytoestrogens thought to help protect against prostate, breast, and colon cancers. However, men should probably avoid supplementing with flaxseed oil: Lab studies suggest it may increase the growth of prostate cancer cells.

Garlic, onions, and scallions: Research in China shows that men who eat more foods in the pungent allium family are less likely to develop prostate cancer.

Green tea: This beverage contains antioxidant compounds called polyphenols, which have been shown in lab tests to block the development of prostate cancer.

Be Proactive: Review you food and liquid intake and add those things listed above to your diet, in moderation, if they are not already in it.

Alcohol Poisoning and Your Brain

Dr. Daniel Amen is a psychiatrist with a difference. He uses a brain-scanning technique called *Brain SPECT Imaging*. A SPECT scan shows the underlying cerebral blood flow and consequently metabolic activity patterns of the brain. This is different than say, a CAT scan, because it is not a snapshot of the brain, but rather an ongoing "movie" of brain activity, so can show things a snapshot can't. Dr. Amen's research shows the effects of various drugs on the brain's health and functioning. Here is what he says about the effects of alcohol on your brain:

> One of the most common brain toxins is alcohol. We have seen many alcoholics and they have some of the worst brains we have seen.
>
> Alcohol affects the brain by reducing nerve cell firing; it blocks oxygen getting into the cell's energy centers; and it reduces the effectiveness of many different types of neurotransmitters, especially those involved in learning and remembering.
>
> Alcohol is a double-edged sword; depending upon the quantity of intake. Large amounts of it - four or more glasses of wine, or the equivalent in hard liquor - on a daily basis, increases the risk of dementia. However, it has been found that small amounts - a glass of wine once a week or once a month, but not daily - may reduce dementia by up to 70 percent. The reduced risk seems to be related to the fact that alcohol and cholesterol compete with each other and sometimes it is good for alcohol to win.
>
> Small amounts of alcohol compete with HDL, the good cholesterol, which actually removes the harmful types of cholesterol. When a person drinks a little alcohol, HDL is not allowed to bind to the cell membrane, so it is forced back into the blood stream where it lowers LDL and other

harmful cholesterols. This reduces the person's risk of heart disease, atherosclerosis, and strokes, all of which are known causes for dementia.

A recent study from John's Hopkins reported that even small amounts of daily drinking lowered overall brain size. When it comes to the brain, size matters!

My advice is that small amounts of alcohol after age 25 is okay, but don't push it. Why wait until 25 to drink? The brain is not fully developed until 25, especially in the pre-frontal judgment area of the brain. Why poison it before it has had a chance to fully develop?

Most of us drink alcohol from time to time (or pretty regular-ly!). Men in midlife are statistically more prone to drinking too much than folks at other ages. So if this affects you, put down that glass and say Amen, Dr. Amen!

Be Proactive: Watch your alcohol intake. Start educating your children about what alcohol can do to young brains.

Excerpt taken from Dr. Amen's Newsletter
(http://www.amenclinics.com/newsletter/)

Omega-3 and Winter Blahs (S.A.D.)

The short days and long nights of winter can get to people. Here in Alberta, people used to call the mid-winter depression "cabin fever". More recently it has been known as Seasonal Affective Disorder, or S.A.D. I experienced it more when I lived in Vancouver, BC, where there are heavy, thick clouds a lot of the time during winter.

If you are a victim of low winter moods, increasing your intake of Omega-3 fatty acid may help.

Omega-3 and Omega-6 fatty acids are critical for good health in all kinds of areas... heart, brain, immune system, joints, kidneys, and as I mentioned, mood. We get plenty of Omega-6 fatty acids in a normal diet. In fact we get so much that our omega-6s to -3s ratio is about 10:1, and in some cases as high as 40:1, when it should be closer to 6:1.

Having enough of these fatty acids is critical for proper brain functioning, as our brain is 60% fat. The 'fat phobia' that has raged through our society during the past thirty years means that many people, on low-fat or no-fat diets, are simply not getting enough omega-3 fatty acids. The result is everything from depression and mood swings, to increased rates of Alzheimer's and Parkinson's disease, hypertension, high cholesterol and heart attacks.

Dr. Christiane Northrup, who writes a newsletter for women's health (http://www.drnorthrup.com/), thinks there is a link between fat-free, low omega-3 diets, and the increasing use of anti-depressants such as Prozac and Zoloft.

You can get more omega-3 in your diet in a number of ways:

- Eat meat that is finished on grass. Most of the beef raised in North America is finished in feedlots on a corn or barley diet, which decreases the amount of omega-3 in their meat. You can find farms that sell this kind of product by visiting www.eatwild.com. Another bonus of eating grass-finished meat is it is higher in conjugated linoleic acid (CLA), which has been shown in a number of studies to reduce the risk of cancer.

- Eat a wide variety of dark green leafy vegetables, such as kale, collards, dandelion greens, and broccoli.
- Eat cold-water fish regularly. It is best if it is not farm-raised, as farm-raised fish are given a diet of manufactured feed that causes them to have lower levels of omega-3 in their oil.
- Avoid partially hydrogenated fats, such as shortening, margarine, non-dairy creamers and pre-package baked goods. Margarine is no longer thought to be as healthy as butter, and besides, butter tastes better. (Some of the new margarines that are free of trans-fat are said to be okay, but I say why eat that stuff when you can have butter?)
- Take a fish oil supplement. A number of studies show that fish oils, which contain omega-3 fatty acids, can help with mood and cognitive abilities.

Be Proactive: Investing more time in your long term health means investing time now in becoming an educated shopper and moving outside the milieu of your local grocery store. Consider what you can do to add some of the suggestions above to your eating plan.

Sunshine and Prostate

I have been reading in health newsletters recently about how our expert-induced fear of sunshine these days might be a little over the top. In fact some say the vitamin D we get from having sunshine on our skin (not blocked by sunscreen) actually helps fight cancer! These folks quickly caution that we shouldn't immediately go out and sunbathe for hours on end, but rather it is good to get, say, 15 minutes a day of direct sun exposure on our bare skin.

Now some California researchers have found that the more sun a man is exposed to, the lower his risk of advanced prostate cancer. The researchers surveyed 450 white men between the ages of 40 and 79, who had been diagnosed with advanced prostate cancer between July 1997, and February 2000. These men were compared to 455 men the same age without prostate cancer.

They all filled out lengthy questionnaires, which included a history of exposure to the sun. Along with the questionnaires, researchers measured the men's exposure to UV rays by comparing skin pigmentation under the upper arm (where the sun doesn't shine), and the middle of the forehead. The difference between the two was used in determining net lifetime exposure to the sun.

The study found that men without prostate cancer had significantly more exposure to the sun. In fact men who worked outside for 15 hours or more per day (what kind of job sees you doing that?) had the lowest risk of prostate cancer.

For desk-riders the news isn't so good. The amount of time the average man reported biking, walking or doing chores outside didn't appear to help. It seems as though you have to get more sun than that. Just the same ... if you have been worried about going out in the sun for even a few minutes, relax, it will probably do you more good than harm.

Be Proactive: Shine a little sun on your prostate. Well... Not directly on it!

Burnt Offerings and Rectal Cancer

There's nothing a guy likes more than being King of the Barbeque. However, the average barbeque king tends to overcook the meat!

A United States Department of Agriculture study published in the April 2004 issue of the *Journal of Nutrition* found no link between eating red or white meat and rectal cancer. However, it did find a link when males ate red or white meat that was cooked well done. The scientists concluded that the cancer risk comes from substances formed when meat is cooked at higher temperatures. Two heat-related compounds, HCAs (carcinogenic heterocyclic amines) and PAHs (polycylic aromatic hydrocarbons) are the main culprits.

Interestingly, no such link was found in females when well done meat was eaten. And women who consumed juice drippings from red meat actually had a lower risk of rectal cancer. The Journal concluded that eating whole muscle meats medium rare may allow you to avoid the health risk altogether.

Be Proactive: Go for medium or medium rare when you're cooking – yes, eat it that way too!

Fasting and a Cleaner Body

Fasting is an ancient spiritual discipline, as well as a health practice. I had an uncle who fasted one day a week all of his adult life. He did it for his health (he lived to 86), but I fast once a year as a spiritual discipline.

A little over twenty years ago I began to get the sense that fasting would be a good thing for me to do, but I didn't know how to go about it. I didn't want to just quit eating and drinking for a few days and try to carry on a normal life, but I didn't want to go out in the woods on my own either. I was pondering what to do when I serendipitously discovered that a friend of mine led fasts. We knew each other in a different context, and I was not aware he did this. I asked him if I might come to a fast he was co-leading with a man from the Saddle Lake Indian Reserve a couple of hours northeast of Edmonton, Alberta, and he said that would be fine. I have fasted every year since.

Here are the steps we go through to get the best results:

- We arrive on Wednesday about midday. There are usually about twelve to fifteen fasters, roughly half men and half women. The women fast in a different area than the men.

- We cut some willows and build little dome-shaped, tarp-covered hogans, in which we will fast.

- Later in the afternoon we have a sweat lodge, then a meal, and then visit till sundown.

- At about 9:30pm we have a Berry Ceremony. It lasts an hour or two and is designed to invite the "grandfathers" (in Christian terms they would be called angels) to help us during the fast, and to guide us toward the answers to the questions we have come to ponder. At the end of this ceremony, the fast has officially begun. We sleep in a tipi in camp that night.

- The next morning we have another sweat lodge, change into our fasting clothes, and are led out to the fasting grounds and installed in our hogans.

- The next three days are spent in contemplation, prayer and meditation. Different fast leaders have different rules for the fast. For example, for the first fourteen years I fasted, we were not allowed to speak to each other, except for a few hours Saturday afternoon, and we were required to stay awake and alert from sundown until sun-up, or until the first bird sang in the morning. We were allowed to have a fire. In more recent years, because a different man was leading the fast, we were allowed to speak to each other throughout the fast, and we were "tied" (with a rope around the outside of the tarp) into our hogans at sundown, and we're allowed to sleep during the night. We let ourselves out after sunup.

- On the morning of the fourth day (Sunday), the leaders of the fast come and hold a pipe ceremony with each fasting participant, then lead us in procession back to the camp where we have another sweat lodge. After the first round of this sweat, water is brought in and we have a drink, which officially ends the fast. We then have another Berry Ceremony, followed by a feast, then go home.

The fast is the spiritual highlight of my year. After a couple of days of no contact with the outside world, my mind starts to slow down, and I feel more tuned in to the spiritual or "unmanifest" world. Having nothing to eat or drink also helps one's mind focus more clearly during prayer and meditation. During the fast, I usually get insights into the proper direction for my life, and things I should focus on in the coming year and beyond.

The fast also has a cleansing effect on my body. By the end of the fast, my eyes are brighter and clearer, and my system feels "cleaner." That being said, fasting is not for everyone. As with all spiritual disciplines, it is best to follow your intuition as to which discipline suits you best. A good book about the various spiritual disciplines one might practice is *Celebration of Discipline: the Path to Spiritual Growth* by Richard J. Foster, 1988.

Be Proactive: Consider if a fast is the right thing for you. Talk to your health advisor. Find a group who fasts, or a buddy to support you through an initial fast of your own design. Use it to purge the toxins from your body, mind and spirit.

Obesity and Type II Diabetes

I took a genetics course in 1966, where I learned that because of the discovery of insulin, half the population would have Type I diabetes at some time in the future because those with the disease would no longer die before they passed on their diabetic genes to their children.

Type II, or adult onset diabetes however, is largely caused by an unhealthy lifestyle that eventually causes the body to become "resistant" to insulin. This worries a lot of middle age men and so it should, especially if you have had a blood test that shows impaired glucose tolerance, or if one of your parents has Type II diabetes. But the good news is it can be prevented. Here are some tips:

- Keep your weight under control. Some studies show you can reduce your risk by losing as little as five to ten pounds. If you already have Type II, you can even control the symptoms by controlling your weight.
- Eat a low-fat diet. And stay away from the high-glycemic carbohydrates such as white flour, white sugar, and in general, highly processed, sweet foods.

- Exercise. A good diet and exercise are the two keys to good health as we age. Some studies even show that any exercise at all lowers the risk of developing Type II diabetes.

Be Proactive: Follow the three suggestions above.

Vitamin B1 and Your Heart

A study published in the January 17, 2006, issue of the Journal of the American College of Cardiology reported that about one in three patients hospitalized with heart failure had deficient levels of thiamine, also known as vitamin B1. Symptoms of thiamine deficiency are similar to symptoms of congestive heart failure and, may worsen existing heart failure.

Researchers measured thiamine levels among 100 heart failure patients and compared them with measurements of fifty healthy people. They found a deficiency of the vitamin in 33 percent of the heart failure patients compared to 12 percent of those without the disease.

Researchers also observed that heart failure may increase the body's need for certain nutrients, so that even people with healthy diets may still come up short on vitamin B1. Multivitamin supplements, even though they have a relatively small dose of thiamine, can protect you from developing a thiamine deficiency, and if you already have congestive heart failure, could make it a bit less severe.

Be Proactive: Start taking a multi vitamin aimed at your age demographic, so that you keep your B1 level where it should be.

Niacin and Alzheimer's

In a new study, people who consume less than 14 mg of the B-vitamin niacin per day were three times more likely to develop Alzheimer's disease. The researchers believe niacin helps maintain normal neural function.

To get enough niacin, try to get the recommended daily dose of 16 mg (14 mg for women) from niacin-rich foods, which include fortified cereal (20 mg per cup), lean poultry (11.8 mg per half-breast) and canned tuna (11.3 mg per three ounces). You can usually get enough niacin just from eating a varied diet.

And here's a tip ... this handy B vitamin can help level out your mood as well, if you are under stress and having wild mood swings. But if you do that, take niacinamide, not niacin, as large doses of niacin will give you hot flashes and make you feel all prickly and uncomfortable. Niacinamide won't, and they both do the same job.

When my first wife died, my mood was all over the place and my brother-in-law, who is a psychiatric nurse and bush pilot (interesting combination!) suggested I take niacinamide. It helped.

Be Proactive: Get your niacin level checked and if you are not getting those 16 mg a day up your intake of niacin rich foods.

Vitamin D and Good Health

When I was a kid, we were given cod liver oil capsules at school, and we got cod liver oil by the spoonful at home. It tasted REALLY bad, but my parents said it was necessary because we needed sunshine vitamin D, and in the winter, there wasn't much sunshine.

By the time I was in junior high, we were not taking cod liver oil any more. I guess people thought we got enough some other way, or maybe we whined and complained enough that our parents gave up.

However, an article in the Canadian national paper, *The Globe and Mail* by Martin Mittelstaedt, Apr. 28, 2007 made me take notice. It basically said that vitamin D is a very powerful ally in maintaining health, and that most people don't have enough in their blood streams, because they do not get enough sunshine: "One survey published in 2001 estimated office- and homebound Canadians and Americans spend 93 per cent of waking time in buildings or cars, both of which block ultraviolet light."

Of course in recent years everyone has been positively panicky about getting too much sunshine for fear of getting skin cancer, but some experts say that is WAY out of line. Here is an excerpt taken from the article.

> The sun advice has been misguided information "of just breathtaking proportions," said John Cannell, head of the Vitamin D Council, a non-profit, California-based organization.

> Here is another quote from the Globe and Mail story:

> For decades, researchers have puzzled over why rich northern countries have cancer rates many times higher than those in developing countries - and many have laid the blame on dangerous pollutants spewed out by industry.

> But research into vitamin D is suggesting both a plausible answer to this medical puzzle and a heretical notion: that cancers and other disorders in rich countries aren't

caused mainly by pollutants but by a vitamin deficiency known to be less acute or even non-existent in poor nations.

Those trying to brand contaminants as the key factor behind cancer in the West are "looking for a bogey man that doesn't exist," argues Reinhold Vieth, professor at the Department of Nutritional Sciences at the University of Toronto and one of the world's top vitamin D experts. Instead, he says, the critical factor "is more likely a lack of vitamin D."

What's more, researchers are linking low vitamin D status to a host of other serious ailments, including multiple sclerosis, juvenile diabetes, influenza, osteoporosis and bone fractures among the elderly.

Not all health experts agree with the claim that vitamin D can help prevent cancer, but apparently they will get a comeuppance in June when U.S. researchers will announce the first direct link between cancer prevention and vitamin D. Their results are impressive. A four-year clinical trial of 1,200 women found those taking vitamin D had 60 percent fewer cancer incidences than those who didn't take it. This is twice the impact on cancer attributed to smoking. And it was achieved with an over-the-counter supplement that cost pennies a day.

How Much Vitamin D Do You Need?

Recommendations vary, but it appears you have to take a LOT before it will harm you. I read on a medical chat group about a couple of people who had vitamin D toxicity, but they were taking a million international units per day!

The conclusion of the 334 scientists from 23 countries at the meeting in Victoria, British Columbia in April, 2006 was that governmental guidelines for daily vitamin D requirements in all countries are too low, and out of step with current research findings.

Dr. Andrew Weil, a well-known M.D. who is very strong on health maintenance, recommends 1,000 IU of vitamin D per day, based on recent research.

All the research I read says we do not get enough vitamin D from foods, including those such as milk, which are 'fortified', and it suggests you look for supplements that provide vitamin D3 (choleciferol) rather than D2 (ergocalciferol).

Be Proactive: Get out there and get some sunshine. Consider Vitamin D supplements.

Relaxation Exercise and Wellness

Here's an exercise that Adair Wilson Heitmann, director of the *Center for Creativity and Wellness* in Fairfield, Connecticut recommends. To quickly release tension Heitmann advises a technique derived from the Japanese healing art called jin shin jyustsu. While it's best to do this in a restful place where you can shut your eyes, it's not necessary. Heitmann says you can do it any time you're feeling out of balance. It's especially good for nervous airplane travelers.

Here's what you do:

"Wrap your entire right hand around your left thumb, as if your hand were a tortilla wrapping the thumb. Hold that for one to five minutes, and then alternate left hand on right thumb. Go through each of your fingers this way, always alternating hands.

The energy flow through each of the fingers has a particular association -- the thumb with worry... the index finger with fear... the middle finger with anger... the ring finger with grief... and the pinky with pretense or façade."

Heitmann adds, "Although this method is excellent for releasing tension in general, if you are experiencing one of these aspects in particular, you can hold the corresponding digits of each hand, alternating as described, to find relief."

SECTION SIX

IS A HARLEY REALLY PRACTICAL?

Just Imagine...

Goals

I joined a mastermind group (there are five of us), and in one of our meetings we were talking about goal setting. One member, Jamie, said he heard a speaker many years ago say that goal setting just sets you up for failure.

The experts tell you to make a list of your goals and then set a deadline for when you will accomplish each one. The problem is that in reality, even if you do set goals, either you don't reach them at all, or don't reach them by the deadline, which makes you feel badly. You may even start to see yourself as a failure unable to accomplish the important things in your life.

A better way is to have a life direction or mission, and maybe establish a theme for the year, with some actions that will move you toward that theme. Then instead of establishing completion deadlines such as, "I will achieve this goal by March 3," use instead "I wonder" phrases, as in, "I wonder how long it will take me to _____?"

Elizabeth and I have used "I wonder" in times of financial stress, and it is interesting how it changes the psychological tone of the situation. Instead of saying, "I don't know how we are going to get through the month end," we would say, "I wonder where the money is coming from to get through the month end." We then felt far more optimistic, which made it easier to do what was necessary to come up with the month-end cash.

Be Proactive: Go over any goals you set that are already past deadline. Reconsider if they still have merit. Prioritize them in order of which is the most important to achieve, then come up with some "I wonder" phrases that will remove the fear of failure and move you closer to making it happen.

Letting Go

I learned an interesting meditation in the book *The Seven Stages of Money Maturity* by George Kinder. The idea is to "let the thoughts go, let the feelings be."

When you are feeling worried or fearful or any other strong emotion, especially a negative one, you usually attach a thought to it. If you are not sure where your next money will come from, you might be worried and think *I'm in trouble, I'm short of money.*

In the meditation, you simply let any thoughts go about why you are worried (I am short of money), and put your attention on the feeling. You just be with the feeling, wherever it is in your body, and just notice the feeling. (How does your stomach/chest/gut etc. feel when you are worried?) You don't try to do anything with the feeling. Just put our consciousness on it and experience it fully.

As you do this, you 'make friends' with the feeling, and realize it comes from somewhere deep and long ago (an echo of another experience entirely). When certain situations (fear of not having enough money) call *it* forth, you think that is the cause of the feeling.

I did this mediation a while back for about 15 minutes. I was feeling a little anxious about money, and had a 'heightened' feeling in my chest, and I couldn't tell whether it was anxiety or some form of subtle excitement.

As I meditated and went into the feeling, there was a kind of darkness in it that eventually began to lift. It was as though a dark blanket rose up out of my heart, up through my throat, and on up and out the top of my head. I still had the feeling of anxiety/excitement in my chest, but it felt okay to have it there.

Be Proactive: Next time you have a negative feeling, sit quietly and get in touch with your body. Identify how it feels and focus on the physical symptoms of your feeling. Breathe deeply into those areas. You should get some relief almost immediately.

Planning Your Time

Allan Savory is a friend of mine, and one of the sharpest, most innovative and fearless men I know. He developed "Holistic Management" (www.holisticmanagement.org), which is by far the most effective decision-making framework I have ever seen. I have taught it to hundreds of small business owners, especially farms and ranches, and it invariably improves the owners' quality of life; improves their profits, often dramatically; and guides them in managing for a sustainable resource base (land, people, technology).

Allan can get more done in a day than most of us can in a week. He uses a simple approach to time management that anyone can use to good effect. Here are the principles:

ANY TIME MANAGEMENT PLAN MUST CONTAIN TWO ELEMENTS: HABIT and TRUST

A Planning Method

- Keep your planning calendar (palm pilot, daytimer, whatever) in your office or home, but never take it with you. Every evening before going to bed, figure out what will be on your 'to do' list the next day, write it on a piece of paper and stick it in your pocket.

- As you go through the day and people ask you to do something, NEVER say yes. Write it on the paper and tell them you will get back to them after you consult your calendar. This also goes for ideas you get through the day, jot them down and consult your calendar.

- When you get back to your planner, evaluate whether these requests should be scheduled, and if so, give them a place in your calendar.

I hear you say, "That's fine, but what about when my boss tells me I must do a certain task, even if my calendar is already full. What do I do then?"

I have no simple answer for that, but if you truly have a full calendar and the boss wants you to add to it, ask him/her what should come out in its place. Also... strenuously avoid committing to anything that you don't HAVE to do. (The above process should help in that regard.)

Ideally you should work first on the 'urgent and important' things, then on the 'important but not urgent', and spend little or no time working on things that are 'urgent but not important'. Unfortunately, my observation is (at least in my case) that we can get awfully busy working in the 'urgent but not important' field of endeavour. This is especially so as we get more and more technology (i.e. data flooding into our lives, much of which is interesting, but not important.).

It is also one's default mode for procrastination, when the urgent and important is just too big or scary feeling for you to want to tackle it. You can spend a lot of time doing unimportant things, such as clearing all the silly jokes passed on by friends out of your email.

Be Proactive: Try out the planning method described above. Give yourself permission to say "NO" to things you don't want to do.

Safeguarding Your Identity

A few years ago I got a credit card bill with about $1200 worth of charges for things I hadn't bought. I phoned the merchants who sold the goods (two computer stores - one in Toronto and one in Montreal), and asked what had been bought, and where it had been sent. They told me, and gave me an address in Vancouver (I was living there at the time).

I called the police and with the address they were able to make an arrest. They told me to phone my credit card company, which I did. The company took the charges off my bill, and presumably took some kind of action against the thief. That was my first (and so far only) experience with what has come to be called identity theft. It shook me up, and I began to be more careful with my private information.

On my computer, I now have a router, which acts as a physical firewall; and software firewall; a program that scans every email, and anything I download from the net, and scans my whole hard drive every morning for viruses, worms, trojans and any other nasty little programs the crooks of the world employ; plus I use a program that creates complex passwords, and fills in forms and passwords on the net.

I also shred, with a confetti-style shredder, any paper that has any kind of sensitive information on it.

Identity Theft Insurance

There are articles almost daily in the major newspapers about how identity theft is becoming an epidemic. Experts figure as many as one in five Canadians will become victims of identity theft in one form or another. I have read estimates as high as one in four in the US.

There are several types of identity theft:
- Credit card.
- Bank account.
- Medical (somebody else runs up big bills in your name).
- Criminal (a bad guy gets caught, gives your name, skips bail, and the next time you get pulled over for a speeding ticket, you go to jail).
- Loans - people buy houses, etc. in your name, or transfer the title of your house to someone else and then take out a loan against it, which you end up paying off.
- Drivers license, passport - people use your identity to do bad stuff.

- Employment - people get jobs in your name, using your SSN or SIN, you pay the taxes.
- Social security or SIN number - people get your pension, and other government benefits.

I don't want to be a victim of any of the above, so I bought the *Identity Theft Shield* from Pre-Paid Legal Services Inc. (Pre-Paid Legal is a network marketing company that has been in business for more than thirty years, and is listed on the NYSE.)

With their Identity Theft Shield, a trained expert will work on your behalf to help correct identity theft issues you have with affected agencies and institutions, including:

- Credit card companies
- Financial institutions
- Credit repositories
- Phonebusters
- Reporting Economic Crime Online (RECOL)
- Internet Fraud Complaint Centers (IFCC)
- Passport Canada
- Law enforcement personnel and other organizations that may maintain information about you

Fraud alert notifications will be sent on your behalf to all three credit bureaus and financial institutions when appropriate.

A professional thief can assume your identity in just a few hours, but it can take years for you to restore your credit standing. I don't want to take that chance.

Putting the Seat Down

In midlife your marriage can be at a dissatisfying stage, and you can do little things that irritate each other. This is a time when you need to evaluate what irritants you're adding to the mix and which ones you can take responsibility for removing. For example, if you leave the seat up on the toilet, it creates a possible unpleasant experience for your wife or children, and is usually followed by an unpleasant scene for you. Better to do little things that feel good to each other, and putting the seat down is an easy one you can do.

In leading communication workshops a few years ago, I would explain 'I statements' and 'you statements,' then form small groups and have each group come up with a conflict scenario. A number of different scenarios were acted out, but one that often showed up if women were the majority in the small group was "putting the toilet seat down." Some acting was hilarious, but the message was serious ... it is VERY uncomfortable to sit down on a cold, often wet, toilet bowl, because someone has left the seat up.

I have sat down on such a seat, and perhaps you have too. Women do it more often, and they REALLY HATE IT.

It is a simple courtesy a man can extend to others who use the toilet. As my dear old Dad says, there is no excuse for leaving the seat up. If you are not in the habit of putting the toilet seat down, start doing so.

Be Proactive: Think of some of the things you are doing that irritate your partner and decide if they are more important to you than having more peace in your life. If not, dump them and feel the calm descend.

Shopping With Your Wife

From time to time you may be invited to go shopping with your wife. Often it's quite a spell before the invitation is extended again, because it turns out the shopping trip is not much fun for either party. The woman ends up frustrated and angry, and you end up bored, nervous and angry.

It CAN be fun to shop with your wife, if you understand the difference in how men and women shop. Now I understand what I am about to say is a generalization, and you may be thinking *that's not how it is with Betty and me*, but I believe what I am about to tell you is GENERALLY true.

When men go shopping, we know what we want, we know roughly where to get it, and we go get it. For us shopping is much like making a phone call:

Rrriinnng...

"Hello."

"Fred?"

"Yah."

"Tom."

"How's it going?"

"Good. Want to play golf on Saturday?"

"Sure. What time."

"I have a tee time at 7:00 at the Golden West course."

"OK. See you there."

When we go shopping, we hunt down what we want, buy it, and go home.

Women, on the other hand, experience shopping more as a sensory event. They like to look at things, feel them, take their time, and savour the moments. A woman would never consider buying the first purse, or blouse, or whatever, she finds, even if it is pretty much what she is looking for. She wants to be sure she is getting the most flattering outfit at the best price, so she likes to compare things and get feedback on how things look on her.

Now, put these two shopping styles together, and you have the makings of one of those "marital discord" events we experience from time to time, where we might be having a little hot tongue and cold shoulder for supper.

Here's the scenario:

It's Saturday, and there is some family shopping to do, but it won't take too long, and Linda is thinking it might be nice for her and Ted to do it together. She pictures them wandering around the mall a bit, getting the things they need, and maybe going for coffee in the new coffee boutique that just opened up.

Linda invites Ted to come along. Ted ascertains that they don't have a lot to buy, so says okay, thinking they will be home in time to catch the afternoon game on TV, and maybe he'll still have time to change the oil in the Chev before supper.

Off they go. Linda is feeling good. It's been a while since she and Ted spent much time together. On the way into the mall she takes his hand. Ted feels good too. It's nice to spend a little time with Linda.

The first thing on the list is some panty hose for Linda. Ted doesn't know much about panty hose, but how hard can it be?

"What colour are you looking for?"

"Something in a kind of mocha tone."

Ted is not sure what a mocha tone is, but there are many shades of brownish-looking panty hose in the shelves. At least half look like they could be mocha tone. He picks out a couple and shows them to Linda.

"No, that's not quite it. A little darker, I think."

His next offerings are too dark, then too brown, and so it goes.

Pretty soon Ted sits down in the chair conveniently located for men who are shopping with their wives, and waits. Not too patiently.

Linda now feels pressured. The fun is starting to wear off.

It's not hard to imagine how the rest of the trip goes, and needless to say, they don't go for the coffee and intimate chat Linda first imagined.

Now, this COULD have been a good trip for both of them if Ted had been aware that Linda was seeing it as an outing, maybe a chance to spend some time together and talk. He could have treated it as the "date" that Linda was imagining, and simply remained relaxed and cheerful through the shopping part, and maybe bought Linda a little treat along with the coffee. Who knows what might have happened in bed later as well.

Be Proactive: Here are a couple of tips that can help you have a good shopping outing with your wife:

- Determine what you are getting into, and what your wife is picturing the trip to be before you go (it might be good to ask for clarity. Maybe she just wants help getting the shopping done).
- Be prepared to give the time willingly and cheerfully. Think of it as something nice you are doing for your wife. Don't expect her to repay it. She might even think she is doing you a favour by inviting you to come! It's part of marriage. Besides, if you relax and go with the flow, it might be nice for you too.

- If you are pretty sure you can't make the trip pleasant for both of you (Elizabeth doubts a man can truly enjoy this kind of shopping), do both of you a favour and decline graciously. Maybe offer to do something else she will appreciate that you CAN do willingly.

Where There Is a Will, There Is a Way

A surprisingly small percentage of adults (some say as few as 20%) have written wills. If you are single with no dependents, and have few possessions, there may be some excuse for this, but beyond that, there is none, as far as I am concerned.

A will is a way of looking after your family's needs when you are gone. It is also a way of making sure your wishes for what happens to your estate are carried out, and it is a way to keep your family from getting into fights that could tear it apart. They say "money makes people funny," and I have heard many stories of family members doing all kinds of sneaky things, such as stealing heirlooms and emptying bank accounts, when a parent dies, before the siblings even know what's happening.

Denying Death?

Some psychologists say refusing to write a will is a form of 'death denial', as though writing it will somehow either hasten your death, or at least make you face your mortality. Elizabeth and I wrote our wills shortly after we got married, and I suppose it did make us think a bit about our death, but by the time you reach midlife, chances are you are going to be considering it anyway. If not, you might be in denial, and be prone to acting as though you will never die by trying to stay "young and hip" when you aren't any more. (Hip, maybe; young at heart, hopefully; but not young.)

If you do not have a will, I strongly urge you to write one. Get some legal advice, so it is done properly. If you hand write it (this is called a holograph will), which is a poor idea but could be done in an emergency, it must all be in your handwriting, not partly typed and partly written, in order to be a legal will.

Be Proactive: If you love your family, write a will.

Other Potential Biker Issues

Dumping Your Load

I don't know anybody who doesn't have too much to do. And it seems at midlife you are busier than ever, with work, kids, and perhaps the needs of aging parents. I talk to many men who feel as though they can never relax because the work is never done.

I learned long ago that the work *will* NEVER all be done, so when I stop for the day, I can usually leave what's unfinished for tomorrow without worrying about it too much.

Here is a little story that makes that point from *Who Ordered This Truckload of Dung? Inspiring stories for welcoming life's difficulties* by Ajahn Brahm:

What's Done Is Finished

The monsoon in Thailand is from July to October. During this period, the monks stop traveling, put aside all work projects, and devote themselves to study and meditation. The period is called Vassa the Rains Retreat.

In the south of Thailand some years ago, a famous abbot was building a new hall in his forest monastery. When the Rains Retreat came, he stopped all work and sent the builders home. This was the time for quiet in his monastery.

A few days later a visitor came, saw the half-constructed building and asked the abbot when his hall would be finished. Without hesitation, the old monk said, "The hall is finished."

"What do you mean, 'The hall is finished'?" the visitor replied, taken aback. "It hasn't got a roof. There are no doors or windows. There are pieces of wood and cement bags all over the place. Are you going to leave it like that? Are you mad? What do you mean, 'The hall is finished'?"

The old abbot smiled and gently replied, "What's done is finished," and then he went away, to meditate.

That is the only way to have a retreat or to take a break. Otherwise our work is never finished.[13]

Be Proactive: Don't let your work own you. Find a method that allows you to dump it at the end of the day, for the weekend, over your holidays. Free up your time and focus so that you can give meaning to the other parts of your life.

Joining the Sandwich Generation

My mother died at age 85 and spent her last couple of years in long-term care. She was in a wheel chair for about three years

---

[13] Brahm, Ajahn; *Who Ordered This Truckload of Dung?: Inspiring Stories for Welcoming Life's Difficulties*; Wisdom Publications; Somerville, MA; 2005.

before that, and my dad who was 89 when she went in had been looking after her at home, with the help of some wonderful home care mostly paid for by the Alberta government.

It was one of those emotional times for my brother, two sisters and me, when the woman who used to be so big and important and powerful and competent in our lives was now basically helpless.

Of course, we were not alone in this. Here is a quote from the Herman Trend Alert, January 26, 2005 (www.hermangroup.com/alert/archive_1-26-2005.html):

> Boomers are preparing for at least a decade of caring for parents, children, and themselves – at the same time. This burden will force them to continue working to produce the income needed to meet their widespread obligations. A recent survey conducted by the National Partnership for Women and Families found that nearly two-thirds of Americans under age 60 expect to be responsible for the care of an elder relative within the next 10 years. About half of US workers are raising children under the age of 18.

One of the big challenges is finding a good nursing home, or other long-term care facility. We hear all kinds of horror stories about old people being warehoused and ignored, or worse, but most of us don't know what to look for when choosing a place for our parent(s).

A quick search in the library catalogue using the term "nursing home" brings up quite a few titles, but one book that seems to be very thorough, and I first heard of when it was recommended in the CARP (Canadian Association of Retired Persons) magazine about a year ago, is *A Spy In The Nursing Home*. The author,

Eileen Kraatz, has worked in nursing homes, and knows what goes on behind the scenes.

If you are in the sandwich generation, and are facing the turmoil of having to move a parent to a nursing home, this book can be very useful. Also, don't take it for granted that once you have found a home you like that you can actually get your parent into it any time soon. There are waiting lists for almost every long-term care facility in Canada. If you can see that your parent is failing, it may not hurt to find out the timelines on the waiting list for the facility you choose. So, if one or more of your parents is becoming part of the "frail elderly," don't get caught unprepared. Do your homework up front, so that you have information at hand to offer them when they are suddenly faced with making a choice. A fall can change their lives in minutes – and yours!

The 4-Hour Workweek

If you are working too hard, and putting off what you would really like to do till some future, unknown date, you will find *The 4-Hour Workweek* [14] useful and exciting. The Author, Timothy Ferriss, has been living the life he writes about for the past five years.

He pretty much guarantees that if you follow the directions in the book, you can literally do whatever you want, and have as much money as you need to do it. Ferriss maintains that our society's current plan for success – get an education, get a job, work long hours for 40 years so you can finally do what you want

---

[14] Ferriss, Timothy; *The 4-Hour Workweek*; Crown Publishers, New York, 2007.

- is all wrong. He gives a literal road map for liberating yourself so you can do what you want now.

One of his suggestions is that you sit down and clearly analyze the fears that hold you back from carrying out some of your dreams. Maybe you want to take three months off and travel in Central America, but you 'know' you can't do it right now. The "timing is wrong," or "you can't afford it," or ... you name it.

He says if you really look at your fears (i.e. excuses), and write down the worst-case scenario, you will find it is not anywhere near as bad as you think. I can attest to that. When I thought of quitting my job as a CBC TV news reporter when I was in my early 40s to go back to university, it seemed daunting. What would I do for money? Maybe I would go bankrupt, have to quit school, lose my house, etc., etc.

As it turned out, about the time I started back at university, my ex-wife said she wanted a divorce, we ended up selling the house anyway, and I had to move into an apartment. It was worse than I imagined! But it really wasn't all that bad in reality. I finished my Master's degree, and started teaching Holistic Management, which I loved.

I got a note just last week from a subscriber who has just quit his job with a cable company, and become the Public Affairs Coordinator with the local Habitat For Humanity chapter. It's a big change, but fits more with what his soul calls him to be.

Many years ago I met a couple who sold their house, car, and other accoutrements, and moved to New Zealand for a year. He was a teacher, and they went as part of a teacher exchange. They had a wonderful time, and when they came back, they both went back to work (she was a nurse), and in no time bought another house, car, and the other stuff they had let go. The only difference

I could see between them and the other teachers I knew was that they had a big adventure, and the others didn't.

Think about what you want to be able to say you did at the end of that 40 year cycle. Then make it part of your life now. Get more out of living, and don't work so hard for it – or so long!

Looking to Retirement

Retirement is either coming up or here for most readers. I thought about some questions I needed to ask myself for my retirement. Here is what I came up with. I thought you might find them useful...

1. What do I do with my life? How do I find meaning?
2. How much money do I need and where will it come from?
3. How long will I live? (i.e. how much longer do I have? You can get a pretty good idea by using the calculator at http://calculator.livingto100.com/calculator.)
4. How long till I retire? (How many more pay cheques?)
5. What changes do I have to/want to make in my lifestyle?
6. Where will I live? How will I figure that out?
7. If my wife is working, when will she retire?
8. What will I do while she is still working?
9. Who does the cooking and housework if I am retired and she is working?
10. How do we talk to each other about this stuff?

Take time to sit down and ask yourself some of these questions. Once you know the answers, put them in writing – goals happen five times faster when written down. Get it sorted out in your own mind before you have that talk with your spouse/partner – so that you can present it clearly and convincingly.

Rethinking Your Money Needs

We are an incredibly affluent society, but we are less happy than we used to be. In fact between 1970 and 1990, per capita consumption in the U.S. rose 45%, but quality of life, as measured by the American index of Social Health dropped by 51%. (Figures from a story in the Seattle Post-Intelligencer, January 14, 1992.)

There are plenty of other statistics to show the same thing. People have consistently reported less satisfaction with their lives over time during the past forty years. But here is the interesting thing... when asked what it would take to make their lives better, they say, "More money."

Joe Dominguez and Vicki Robin who wrote *Your Money or Your Life: Transforming Your Relationship with Money and Achieving Financial Independence*, (which for my money is the best book ever written on personal financial management), gave many public seminars on personal financial management during the 1970s and 1980s. They would ask seminar participants to rate themselves on a happiness scale of 1 (miserable) to 5 (joyous), with 3 being "can't complain", and then they correlated their figures with their incomes. In a sample of more than 1,000 people, from both the United States and Canada, the average happiness score was consistently between 2.6 and 2.8 (not even a 3!), whether the person's income was less than $1,000 per month, or more than $4,000 per month.

On the same audience survey sheets, Dominguez and Robin would ask "How much money would it take to make you happy?" The answer: "50 to 100% more than I have now."

After reading their book, Elizabeth and I began to pay more attention to how much fulfillment we got from the money we spent, and found we could cut down significantly on spending and still feel just as happy, if not more so.

Understanding that money represents life energy, and every time you spend money you are giving away your life energy might help you to pay more attention to your spending habits. When you are about to buy something, especially an impulse item, ask yourself, "Is this going to give me my life energy's worth?" It will help you cut down on unnecessary expenditures.

As you age, the things that used to give you a big "fulfillment hit" are different than they were when you were younger. Paying attention to what you need for fulfillment now, which might come more from inside you rather than from a store (yes, even a hardware store), could save you a lot of money. With less money-spending stress, life is more fun!

The Road Less Travelled

One of Robert Frost's most famous poems is "A Road Not Taken":

TWO roads diverged in a yellow wood,
And sorry I could not travel both
And be one traveler, long I stood
And looked down one as far as I could
To where it bent in the undergrowth;

Then took the other, as just as fair,
And having perhaps the better claim,
Because it was grassy and wanted wear;
Though as for that the passing there
Had worn them really about the same,

And both that morning equally lay
In leaves no step had trodden black.
Oh, I kept the first for another day!
Yet knowing how way leads on to way,
I doubted if I should ever come back.

I shall be telling this with a sigh
Somewhere ages and ages hence:
Two roads diverged in a wood, and I—
I took the one less traveled by,
And that has made all the difference.

When I read this poem, it reminds me of the choices we make all the time. Frost couldn't see where either road led, but one was less travelled, and he took it, "And that has made all the difference."

My interpretation is that he took the road his soul called him on. He chose the poet's road or his right livelihood. We often decide to take the main road of the safety of "real" jobs, even though we don't know where that road is taking us either. We think if everybody is going on it, or our parents, or teachers, or guidance counsellors think it is good, it must be right.

But we are middle-aged adults now, and perhaps we are disillusioned with the decision a 17-year-old made on the advice of those who "knew better", but didn't really "know him".

And now we come to another intersection, when we must again decide which road to take.

It can be unsettling, frightening, exhilarating, and challenging to take "the road less travelled by". But my experience is if we choose the road we are called to, our life will be fuller and more satisfying than we can imagine.

I chose my "road less travelled" when at age 42 I went back to university to study what came to be called "sustainable agriculture." It led me to learn a whole new way of making decisions, called Holistic Management; and to teaching hundreds of farm and ranch families how to take better care of their land, while making more profit and enjoying higher quality of life.

I couldn't see any further down my road than Frost could his. And I admit the transition was financially frightening. Yet, once I was up and running, my choice was rewarding in every way and it has made all the difference.

The "road not taken" is still out there. Who knows, I may find myself at the beginning of it someday – or not.